MAINERS
IN THE
CIVIL WAR

Harry Gratwick

Published by The History Press
Charleston, SC 29403
www.historypress.net

Copyright © 2011 by Harry Gratwick
All rights reserved

Front cover image: Courtesy of the Maine Historic Preservation Commission and the Library of Congress, Prints and Photographs Division.
Back cover image: Courtesy of the Library of Congress, Prints and Photograph Division, and the Maine Memory Network.

First published 2011
Second printing 2013

Manufactured in the United States

ISBN 978.1.59629.962.7

Library of Congress Cataloging-in-Publication Data

Gratwick, Harry.
Mainers in the Civil War / Harry Gratwick.
 p. cm.
Includes bibliographical references.
ISBN 978-1-59629-962-7
1. Maine--History--Civil War, 1861-1865--Biography. 2. Maine--Biography. 3. Soldiers--Maine--Biography. 4. Governors--Maine--Biography. 5. Women--Maine--Biography. I. Title.
E511.G73 2010
974.1'03--dc22
2010050116

Notice: The information in this book is true and complete to the best of our knowledge. It is offered without guarantee on the part of the author or The History Press. The author and The History Press disclaim all liability in connection with the use of this book.

All rights reserved. No part of this book may be reproduced or transmitted in any form whatsoever without prior written permission from the publisher except in the case of brief quotations embodied in critical articles and reviews.

The idea for this book came from my wife, Tita, to whom I am grateful for her many helpful suggestions as well as for her patience and confidence in my efforts. Throughout the process, she has been my source of support and edification. I dedicate this book to her with my love and appreciation.

The names of the twenty-four men "Who Gave their Lives in Defense of their Country in the Great Rebellion" are inscribed on a monument on Vinalhaven Island's village green.

Contents

Acknowledgements	7
Introduction	9
1. The Politicians	**13**
Lincoln's First Vice President: Hannibal Hamlin	13
The Wartime Governors: Israel Washburn, Abner Coburn and Samuel Cony	18
2. From Generals to Governors	**25**
The Thirty-Second Governor: Joshua Chamberlain	25
The Thirty-Fifth Governor: Seldon Connor	31
The Thirty-Eighth Governor: Harris M. Plaisted	35
3. Soldiers, Sailors and Marines	**39**
Generals in Blue: Rufus Ingalls and Oliver O. Howard	39
The "Prohibition Regiment" and General Neal Dow	51
The Admiral: Henry Knox Thatcher	57
Two Skippers: The Craven Brothers	63
The Marine: Charles Heywood	72

Contents

4. Three Islanders Go to War	**79**
Deer Isle's Charles Gray	79
Vinalhaven's Lafayette Carver and Woster Vinal	82
5. Two Confederates	**89**
The Raider: Charles Read	89
A General in Gray: Danville Leadbetter	97
6. Three Daughters of Maine	**103**
The Writer: Harriet Beecher Stowe	104
The Humanitarian: Dorothea Dix	110
The "Saintly" Carpetbagger: Amy Morris Bradley	116
Bibliography	123
About the Author	127

Acknowledgements

This book could not have been written without support from the librarians at the Main Branch of the Free Library of Philadelphia. I am very grateful to them for their assistance in helping me identify and obtain numerous books dealing with Mainers in the Civil War.

In the Interlibrary Loan Department, Sheila Williams, Steven Blowney and Sandy Miller were very obliging in helping me with my numerous requests for out-of-state books. In the Social Science Department, Barbara Pilvin, Peter Lehu, Joseph Wilson, Richard Boardman, Paul Artrip and Jim DeWalt were patient and cooperative by showing me books that were available in the stacks and the main room. In the Prints and Pictures Department, Karen Lightner, Ted Cavanagh and David DuPuy were very accommodating by helping me locate old photos and paintings in their extensive collection of Civil War photos and paintings.

I also would like to thank the following people for their help and advice on specific topics: Matthew Hansbury, collections manager at the General Knox Museum in Thomaston; Richard Lindermann at the Bowdoin College Library; Cory Black at Naval Historical Center in Washington, D.C.; Diane Cobb Cashman, author of *Headstrong*, the biography of Amy Bradley, for her many helpful suggestions about this remarkable woman; Charles J. Torrey, research historian at the Museum of Mobile, Alabama; Diane Hesketh at Androscoggin Historical Society in Auburn; May Billingslea and Robert Quatrano at the Neal Dow Memorial, headquarters of the Maine Woman's Christian Temperance Union, in Portland; Lauri Likoff, editorial director at Infobase Publishing in New York City; Earle Shettleworth, state historian and director of the Maine Historic Preservation Commission; Bill Haviland at

Acknowledgements

the Deer Isle–Stonington Historical Society; Dani Fazio at Maine Historical Society; and Frank Garber at the Chestnut Hill Camera Shop.

Finally, I would like to thank Sue Radley, Bill Chillis, Roy Heisler and Loretta Chillis at the Vinalhaven Historical Society as well as Valerie Morton and Linda Whittington at Vinalhaven Public Library for their generous help and support.

Introduction

Early on the morning of April 12, 1861, a mortar shell arched across the sky and exploded over Fort Sumter in the middle of Charleston Harbor. For the next thirty-four hours, Confederate artillery pounded Federal troops until the fort's commander, Major Robert Anderson, surrendered and evacuated his men. (Remarkably, the only fatality on either side was a mule). The next day, April 15, 1861, President Lincoln called for seventy-five thousand volunteers to expand the sixteen-thousand-man Union army, and the shadow of war spread across the country.

Most Mainers were outraged by the rebellion and responded enthusiastically to the president's call. Maine contributed the largest number of combatants of any state in the Union, in proportion to its population. Estimates range as high as seventy thousand men who were organized into thirty-two infantry regiments, two cavalry regiments and eight artillery batteries. In addition, another five thousand to six thousand men enlisted in the navy and spent the war blockading Southern ports and chasing Confederate raiders across the oceans of the world. Maine was second only to Massachusetts in the number of sailors who served in the Union navy.

One reason Maine responded with such fervor may have been that a native son—who was a former United States senator and the twentieth governor of the state—was now the vice president. Hannibal Hamlin, from Paris Hill, a powerful orator and a strong opponent of slavery, had been selected as Lincoln's running mate in 1860.

The year 2011 marks the 150th anniversary of the beginning of this most deadly of all American wars. At least 618,000 Americans died in the Civil War, and some experts say the toll reached 700,000. The war cost

Introduction

The shelling of Fort Sumter, April 12, 1861. The North, including Maine, reacted quickly to the president's call for volunteers. *Courtesy of Print and Picture Collection, Free Library of Philadelphia.*

Maine dearly. Out of a population of 630,000, almost 9,000 Mainers died in the war. Wounds and/or sickness disabled an additional 11,000 men. These casualties exceed the nation's loss in its wars, from the Revolution through Vietnam.

In 1863, there were eleven regiments of Maine men at the pivotal Battle of Gettysburg where Union forces turned back a Confederate invasion under General Robert E. Lee. Of special note were the actions of Brewer native and future governor Joshua Chamberlain, a language professor from Bowdoin and commander of the Twentieth Maine Infantry Regiment. Chamberlain successfully led the defense of Little Round Top on the second day of the battle.

In all, over thirty men from Maine served as generals in the Union army, including Chamberlain, Rufus Ingalls and Oliver Howard, whose lives will be discussed in this book. Danville Leadbetter, from Leeds, had the unusual distinction of being appointed a brigadier general in the Confederate army. How this came about is an interesting story. Two other generals later became

INTRODUCTION

This rare wood engraving by A.R. Waud is of Maine troops in action. It depicts the First Maine Cavalry (dismounted) skirmishing. It was in the September 5, 1863 issue of *Harper's Weekly*. *Courtesy of Maine Historic Preservation Commission.*

governors of the state: Seldon Connor and Harris Plaisted, who was called a "communist" by an opponent.

Thomaston native Henry Knox Thatcher, a grandson of Washington's secretary of war, Henry Knox, had a distinguished naval career, which culminated in his leading the successful Union assault on Fort Fisher, North Carolina, in 1864. The Craven brothers, Thomas and Tunis, also had long and illustrious careers as naval officers and each performed courageously during the war. Their contributions will be discussed. Commodore James Alden, from Portland, a hero of the Battle of Mobile Bay, was the subject of a chapter in my last book, *Hidden History of Maine*.

When Abraham Lincoln met Harriet Beecher Stowe in 1862, he allegedly said, "So this is the little lady who started this big war." Although not a native of Maine, Stowe wrote the powerful bestseller *Uncle Tom's Cabin*, published in 1852, while living in Brunswick, Maine, where her husband, Calvin, was teaching theology at Bowdoin College. The book has never been out of print.

In several ways, my book continues the "hidden history" theme I wrote about in *Hidden History of Maine*. Individual readers may be familiar with some of the people who are profiled, although other names will be less

INTRODUCTION

recognizable. It is beyond the scope of this book, however, to present an inclusive review of important people from Maine who fought in the war. With the exception of the *Two Confederates* chapter, my focus is on the variety of individuals whose actions influenced the war and the postwar period in Maine and, in some cases, the nation.

Chapter 1

The Politicians

LINCOLN'S FIRST VICE PRESIDENT: HANNIBAL HAMLIN

I am only the fifth wheel of a coach and can do little for my friends.
—*Hannibal Hamlin*

In the nineteenth century, the office of the vice-presidency was considered "a post devoid of power and patronage," according to Maine historian H. Draper Hunt. And yet it is interesting that even in his native state of Maine, Hannibal Hamlin is best remembered as Lincoln's first vice president and not the fact that he was a powerful United States senator for twenty-five years.

Hamlin himself had such a low opinion of the office of vice president that he frequently left Washington to return to Maine to work on his farm. "I neither expected it or desired it," Hamlin wrote to his wife when he was given the news of his nomination in the middle of a card game. "But the decision has been made and as man faithful to the cause, it leaves me no alternative but to accept it." The "cause," of course, was the abolition of slavery.

The fifteenth vice president of the United States was born in 1809, the same year as Lincoln, in the town of Paris Hill, in what was, until 1820, the Province of Maine. Paris Hill is nestled in the western part of the state only a few miles from the New Hampshire border. Hamlin's formal education at Hebron Academy was cut short when his father died in 1829, and he was forced to return home to take charge of the family farm. To supplement his income, he taught at the local school. At one point, Hannibal had to stand up to a bunch of older boys who threatened to "toss their young teacher out the window." "You will find I will be the master," the burly Hamlin announced, and the uprising fizzled out.

The year 1833 was a propitious one for Hamlin. He was admitted to the Maine Bar Association, and he won his first case against prominent local attorney Judge Stephen Emery. Later that year, he married the judge's daughter, Sarah, whom he had been courting for some time. The couple moved to Hampden, south of Bangor, where Hamlin opened a law practice and served as the town's attorney. Four Hamlin children were born while the couple was living in Hamden.

Hamlin's political career began in 1836 when he was elected to the Maine House of Representatives. In 1838, he was elected speaker of the House because of his energy and his ability to get things done. Hamlin moved to the national political stage in 1842 and served two terms in the U.S. House of Representatives. As one who was strongly opposed to the extension of slavery in the territories, he soon found himself a minority in the Democratic Party. When Maine's senator, John Fairfield, died in 1848, Hamlin was chosen by the Maine legislature to fill the vacant seat. Hamlin served out Fairfield's term, and in 1851, he was elected to a full six-year term.

Hannibal Hamlin as a United States senator in 1850. Hamlin served as a senator both before and after the war, for a total of twenty-five years. *Courtesy of the Library of Congress, Prints and Photographs Division.*

Throughout this period, Hamlin was a constant thorn in the side of the proslavery wing of the Democratic Party. He supported the Wilmot Proviso, which would have banned slavery in the territories that were acquired following the Mexican War. There is the story that, while still a congressman, he was meeting with President James Polk when word came that voting for the proviso had begun. Hamlin managed to avoid Polk's delaying tactics and slipped out in time to cast a vote for the bill. Wilmot's measure passed the House but later

The Politicians

failed in the Senate. When he became a senator, Hamlin spoke out against both the Compromise of 1850, which opposed the principles of the proviso, and the 1854 Kansas Nebraska Act, which effectively repealed the 1820 Missouri Compromise.

The year 1856 was momentous for the man who was arguably the most distinguished figure from Maine to appear on the national stage, until Joshua Chamberlain. In April of that year, Hamlin's wife died of tuberculosis. Then, in June, he caused a national sensation by quitting the Democratic Party and joining the newly organized Republican Party. Finally, in September, he married his wife's half sister, Ellen, twenty-five years his junior, who had come to nurse her sick sister.

In November 1856, he was elected the twentieth governor of Maine. Hamlin had not sought the honor and warned his backers that he would also campaign for the Senate. The governorship held no charms. It was a part-time job with a miniscule salary as well as a single-year term. Hamlin was elected to both offices but he was governor for only six weeks. This was part of a private understanding with party officials that, if elected, he would return to the Senate, where he felt he could have more influence on the nation's affairs.

Hamlin's resignation from the Democratic Party caught the attention of the Republican Party leaders in Washington, who were impressed with his courage in the switch. His defection reflected not only his opposition to slavery but also a willingness to risk his political career by joining a party with such a brief history. The result was that, three years later, Hamlin was nominated to run as Abraham Lincoln's running mate. The feeling was that the well-known Hamlin—a strong antislavery, pro-Union figure from the Northeast—would provide a good balance to the ticket with Lincoln, who was born in Kentucky and represented Illinois.

Hamlin correctly predicted that, if the Republicans won the election, "there is going to be a war, and a terrible one, just as surely as the sun will rise tomorrow." Between his and Lincoln's victory in November 1860, and their inauguration in March 1861, seven states seceded from the Union. Five weeks later, Fort Sumter was fired on.

Hamlin quickly became disillusioned with his new job. For the first time in his political career, he had nobody to represent. He had not met Lincoln before the election and although the two men became friends, the president rarely turned to him for advice. Hamlin's only real responsibility was to preside over the Senate, a job he found boring and thus frequently neglected.

One can only speculate as to the exact nature of Lincoln and Hamlin's relationship. Lincoln once told a friend he wasn't worried about assassination.

An 1860 election poster of Hannibal Hamlin with the nominee for president, Abraham Lincoln. *Courtesy of the Library of Congress, Prints and Photographs Division.*

"Do you think that the people in Richmond would like to have Hannibal Hamlin here any better than myself? I have an insurance on my life worth half the prairie land in Illinois." And yet Lincoln is reported to have consulted Hamlin over his choices for cabinet appointments, and he issued the Emancipation Proclamation at Hamlin's urging.

Hamlin apparently had little influence on the president regarding the conduct of the war. We do know that he urged Lincoln to arm African Americans, and that he strongly supported the appointment of Joseph Hooker—who turned out to be a poor choice—as commander of the Army of the Potomac. And Hamlin was constantly upset by the lack of patronage opportunities the vice-presidency gave him. Secretary of the Navy Gideon Welles considered him "rapacious as a wolf" regarding patronage. All of which goes to show how powerless the vice president must have felt in his position.

In 1864, while the Senate was in recess, Hamlin joined the Maine Coast Guard. In June, he reported for duty at Fort McClary in Kittery. At one point, the vice president stood guard for three nights in a row until he was reassigned to the job of company cook. His biographer, H. Draper

The Politicians

Hunt, sums up Hamlin's situation: "Nothing illustrates the insignificance of the Civil War vice-presidency more graphically than the spectacle of the incumbent toting a musket, cooking up fish chowders and generally playing at being a soldier for two months during one of the most critical periods of the war."

Hamlin was dropped from the Republican ticket in 1864. The party wanted to broaden its appeal, and instead, the convention chose Andrew Johnson, a Democrat from Tennessee, to run with Lincoln. The president was already looking toward Reconstruction, and the feeling was that Johnson, who had proved himself a capable wartime governor of occupied Tennessee, would strengthen the ticket. One can only speculate how Reconstruction might have turned out had Hamlin, a Radical Republican, been president instead of the Southern Democrat Johnson, who had all kinds of trouble with Congress, including his own impeachment.

Although disappointed with the choice of his replacement, Hamlin campaigned actively for Lincoln and Johnson. At their inauguration on March 4, 1865, H. Draper Hunt tells us that Hamlin "provided a bottle for his shaky successor who was recovering from a bout of typhoid fever and a hangover from a party the previous evening." Not surprisingly, Johnson's inauguration address was not a success. The *Bangor Jeffersonian* grumbled, "There was not a respectable man in that whole assemblage who did not hang his head for shame at such conduct and on such an occasion. Every decent man in the nation feels disgraced."

Hamlin said goodbye to Lincoln on March 10, "thoroughly disgusted with everything and almost everyone in public life, excepting the President." In mid-April, however, he returned to Washington the minute he heard of the president's assassination and stood beside Johnson at Lincoln's funeral. Incidentally, Hamlin's daughter, Sarah, and son, Charles, were at Ford's Theater the night the president was shot.

Hamlin deplored Johnson's Reconstruction policies, which he believed were turning the Southern states over to unrepentant Confederates. Later he roundly criticized Maine senator William Fessenden's vote to acquit Johnson of "high crimes and misdemeanors" following his impeachment by the House.

By 1868, tired of life as a private citizen, Hamlin ran for the Senate again and was elected to two more terms. Eventually he became chairman of the Senate Foreign Relations Committee. When he retired in 1880, President James Garfield appointed the now elderly Mainer ambassador to Spain, where he served for two years. There is the story of a dinner party in

Madrid when several foreign diplomats were awed by meeting the former vice president. Little did they know Hamlin's low opinion of the "second office of the land."

In 1882, Hamlin returned to his home in Bangor. He had bought an Italianate mansion from which he maintained a behind-the-scenes presence in local and state Republican politics for the rest of his life. He spent his remaining years farming, fishing, reading and attending local reunions of the Grand Army of the Republic. Hannibal Hamlin died of heart failure on July 4, 1891, while playing cards at his club shortly before his eighty-second birthday.

The Wartime Governors: Israel Washburn, Abner Coburn and Samuel Cony

Three governors in five years? The original Maine constitution that was written in 1820 had a one-year gubernatorial term. This was expanded to two years in 1879 and to a four-year term in 1957. Two-term governor Israel Washburn had achieved a degree of national prominence as a congressman and is considered one of the founders of the Republican Party. Abner Coburn was a successful businessman who capably managed the affairs of the state for a year. Samuel Cony served for three terms and guided Maine into the postwar era.

Israel Washburn

Israel Washburn (1813–1883) was a member of a prominent New England family that emigrated from England in the seventeenth century. Washburn's parents moved in 1806 to Maine, where his father became a prosperous businessman and shipbuilder. Washburn received a classical education before deciding on a career in law. He established a thriving practice in Orono in the 1830s before entering politics at the state level in the 1840s. He was elected to the state legislature in 1842 and 1843.

Washburn made an unsuccessful run for Congress in 1848 as a member of the Whig Party. He changed parties in 1850, ran as a Democrat and was elected to the House of Representatives for five consecutive terms from 1851 to 1861. Washburn won his first election by 1,500 votes and proceeded to increase his margin of victory in each of the succeeding elections. While in Congress, he was chairman of the House Ways and Means Committee and the Committee on Elections.

The Politicians

Washburn was a member of Congress when the slavery question became a critical national issue in the 1850s. In 1854, angry over the passage of the Kansas Nebraska Act, Washburn called a meeting of thirty House colleagues to discuss forming what would become the Republican Party. A name was discussed, and, apparently, it was Washburn who suggested "Republican" as an appropriate name for the party. With only one dissenting vote, the idea was accepted. On July 2, 1854, in Bangor, he delivered a powerful antislavery speech where he used the term "Republican," one of the first politicians to do so. Republican referred to a party that would focus on "the welfare of the union," Washburn said. As a result, he is considered one the founders of the Republican Party at both the state and national level.

In September 1860, Congressman Washburn was elected the twenty-third governor of Maine, with a 17,000 majority over Ephraim Smart, the Democratic candidate. A year later, he was elected to a second term. When the war began, Washburn supported Lincoln's call for troops by recruiting, arming and training ten regiments of volunteers. During his second term, Washburn also formed a state coast guard unit to protect the ships, commerce and harbors of Maine. In addition, he raised funds to complete a railroad running from Halifax, Nova Scotia, to Portland, Maine, and for the construction of Fort Popham at the mouth of the Kennebec River.

Israel Washburn was elected the twenty-third governor of Maine. He served two terms at the beginning of the war. *Courtesy of Maine Memory Network.*

Governor Washburn was encouraged to run for a third term, but he declined the nomination. President Lincoln showed his appreciation for Washburn's services by appointing him collector of customs at Portland. He remained in the position from 1863 to 1877, before retiring. Washburn spent the last six years of his life immersed in his writing, lecturing and serving as chairman of the board of trustees of Tufts College. He died in 1883.

Abner Coburn

Israel Washburn was a tough act to follow, but Skowhegan lumber baron, railroad magnate and philanthropist Abner Coburn (1803–1885) was equal to the task. Coburn came to the governorship with relatively little political experience (three terms in the state legislature) but with a reputation as an excellent manager. During the course of his career, he had amassed a fortune through various business ventures, and he was respected throughout the state as a man of integrity and reliability.

Together with Washburn, Coburn had helped found the Maine Republican Party in 1854. In 1862, when Washburn chose not to seek a third term, Coburn was nominated and elected as the twenty-fourth governor of the state. His supporters, mostly Republicans, proclaimed that, during his tenure, Coburn provided Maine with stable and efficient government during what was perhaps the most difficult time (1862–1863) of the war. His biographer Charles E. Williams writes, "At no time were the duties of the Executive more

Abner Coburn was a successful businessman and philanthropist who was the twenty-fourth governor of Maine. *Courtesy of Maine Memory Network.*

delicate and arduous." In his message to the state legislature, Coburn proudly announced, "The patriotism of our state has surpassed the demands which the national exigency has made upon it."

Coburn's detractors, mostly Democrats, used every Northern defeat to embarrass the Republicans during Coburn's one year in office. Although it was not a good year for the Union's armies, Governor Coburn never lost his zeal for promoting the prosecution of the war or his support of President Lincoln.

Coburn left office in January 1864 and spent the remainder of his life as a philanthropist and in pursuit of his various business interests. As a private citizen, the ex-governor was "pre-eminently a public spirited man," wrote Charles E. Williams. Although he lacked a formal education, Coburn spent a great deal of time and money improving the schools and the quality of life for people in his hometown of Skowhegan. In addition, he was a longtime trustee and vice-president of Colby College, where his business acumen and political connections were invaluable.

Abner Coburn's will is significant. With no children of his own, he left the bulk of his estate—worth well over $1 million—to a variety of institutions and charities. Gifts of note included: $20,000 to the Deserving Poor of Skowhegan, $50,000 to the Maine Hospital for the Insane at Augusta, $100,000 to the Portland General Hospital, $100,000 to the Maine College of Agriculture and $200,000 to Colby College. There were numerous other bequests to charities, churches, hospitals and educational institutions, as well as individual bequests to relatives and private citizens.

Abner Coburn died in 1885 at the age of eighty-one. In announcing his death to the legislature, Governor Frederick Robie stated, "His life is a monument of great usefulness, of high public spirit and patriotism."

Samuel Cony

The last of Maine's wartime governors, Samuel Cony (1811–1870), was a late convert to the Republican Party. Coney was born in Augusta, heir to a family that had served the country with distinction since the Revolutionary War. Young Cony graduated from Brown in 1829 and was admitted to the bar in 1832. He opened an office in Old Town and began his political career.

Originally a Democrat, Cony was viewed as a rising star in state politics. At the age of twenty-four, he was elected to the state legislature, and at twenty-eight, he was a member of then governor John Fairfield's executive council. Subsequently he was appointed state treasurer, and in 1854, he was

Samuel Cony was governor of Maine during the last year of the war and presided over Maine's transition to peacetime. *Courtesy of Maine Historic Preservation Commission.*

elected mayor of Augusta. When the Civil War broke out, Cony switched his allegiance to the Republican Party, pledging his "hearty support to every measure calculated to crush the rebellion."

In 1863, Cony was nominated by the Republicans to run for governor, and he easily defeated the Democratic candidate, winning over 57 percent of the vote. As governor, Cony apparently felt considerable pressure to live up to the achievements of his predecessors, Israel Washburn and Abner Coburn. Troops and provisions were raised, and commissions for 1,400 "qualified" officers were granted. As the following proclamation illustrates, Cony also had other worries: "I Samuel Cony, Governor of the State of Maine, call upon all good citizens, magistrates and people, within her limits and in every locality, to make arrangements for the performance of a common duty—the driving back of the rebel foe."

During the course of the war, Maine was occasionally threatened by rumors of Confederate operations in Canada, which provided a staging point for Rebel attacks, a safe haven for escaped Southern prisoners of war as well as a relay point between England and the Confederacy. Each of these threats was of considerable concern to the governor. Cony issued his proclamation in an effort to alert the citizens of Maine to the dangers posed to the state from the other side of the border.

In the summer of 1864, Maine coastal residents noticed numerous "artists" making sketches along the shore. In reality, the more than fifty men were Confederate topographers sent to Maine to map the coastline. Their objective was to find coves and inlets that could be used to land parties of armed men to attack Maine. The alarm was sounded when Cony received a telegram from the United States consul in St. John, New Brunswick, warning him of the plan.

A later telegram warned "a small raiding party left St. John last night to commit depredations on the Maine frontier." The gang of Southerners, headed by a William Collins, was headed for Calais to rob a bank. On July 18, 1864, Collins and three other men were arrested inside a Calais bank. A Confederate flag was found on Collins and, after some prodding, he admitted his Southern sympathies. No connection, however, could be found between the robbers and Confederate operations. The men were therefore tried on a charge of "conspiracy to rob," convicted and sentenced to three years in the Maine State Prison. In November 1864, Collins escaped and returned to New Brunswick.

Subsequent rumors included those of Confederate weapons caches scattered around the North and the names of twenty Rebel agents operating in the Union. Although a major attack from Canada never materialized, the threat was enough to give the citizens of Maine a bad case of the jitters during the latter stages of the war.

In recognition of his eventful and successful first year as governor, Cony was reelected twice more. He was offered renomination for a fourth term, but his health was in decline. In his inaugural address in January 1866, Cony notified the legislature, "At the close of the present year my connection with public affairs will cease and I shall most gladly return to that retirement from which I was called."

With the ending of the war and of Confederate plots, Cony's last term as governor was relatively calm. He enjoyed a well-earned, peaceful retirement for the remainder of his life. Samuel Cony died in 1870, surrounded by his wife and six children.

Chapter 2

From Generals to Governors

THE THIRTY-SECOND GOVERNOR: JOSHUA CHAMBERLAIN

Of the more than thirty Union generals from Maine, there were three men—Joshua Chamberlain, Seldon Connor and Harris Plaisted—who became governors of the state in the years following the war. Three other future governors also fought in the war but at a lower rank: Daniel Davis, Henry Cleaves and Frederick Robie. None of the six was a professional soldier. Each volunteered his services to the Union cause and returned to civilian life after the conflict.

Joshua Chamberlain is without a doubt the outstanding member of the group. His exploits have been well chronicled, including Michael Shaara's book *The Killer Angels* (1976), Ken Burns's Civil War television documentary (1990) and the film *Gettysburg* (1993). The following brief review of Chamberlain's career will indicate how richly he deserved his fame.

Joshua Lawrence Chamberlain was born in 1828 in the farming and shipbuilding community of Brewer, Maine, across the Penobscot River from Bangor. He was named after Commodore James Lawrence, who uttered the immortal words, "Don't give up the ship" in the War of 1812. "Lawrence," as his family called him, came from a long line of soldiers. Two great-great-grandfathers had fought in the Revolution. A grandfather was a colonel in the War of 1812, and his father commanded troops in the undeclared 1839 confrontation with England known as the Aroostook War.

Chamberlain's father encouraged him to enter the army, but his mother wanted him to be a minister. After extended family discussions,

Joshua Lawrence Chamberlain, the thirty-second governor of Maine, joined the army after leaving his teaching position at Bowdoin College. *Courtesy of the Library of Congress, Prints and Photographs Division.*

young Chamberlain entered Bowdoin College in 1848, where he proved to be an excellent student with a particular flare for languages. (Lawrence had already taught himself to read ancient Greek in order to pass the entrance exam.)

At Bowdoin, "Joshua"—as he now referred to himself—met two women who would strongly influence his life. The first was Harriet Beecher Stowe, the wife of college professor Calvin Stowe. As an undergraduate, Chamberlain frequently visited her house to hear readings from her soon-to-be-acclaimed novel, *Uncle Tom's Cabin*. The other woman was his future wife, Francis "Fanny" Adams, the adopted daughter of a local clergyman.

After graduation in 1852, Chamberlain spent three years at the Bangor Theological Seminary preparing to become a missionary. In 1855, however, he had a change of heart and accepted a teaching position at Bowdoin. He married Fanny later that year, and the couple settled into the quiet life of academia. They would have five children.

At Bowdoin, Chamberlain rapidly became the wunderkind of the college faculty. He began as a teacher of rhetoric and eventually went on to teach every subject in the curriculum except for mathematics and science. In addition to English, Chamberlain had become fluent in nine languages: Greek, Latin, Spanish, German, French, Italian, Arabic, Hebrew and Syriac, a middle Aramaic language, all in preparation for what he thought would be his life as a missionary.

When the war broke out in April 1861, Chamberlain was eager to join the Union army, though Bowdoin was reluctant to lose his services. The college finally granted him a paid leave of absence to study languages in Europe. Instead, he enlisted and accepted a commission from Governor Israel Washburn as a lieutenant colonel in the Twentieth Maine Infantry Regiment.

Chamberlain knew little of soldiering, but he learned quickly by observing the regiment's commander, Adelbert Ames, a West Point graduate, transform nine hundred inexperienced men into a disciplined force. Altogether, Chamberlain saw action in twenty-four battles and numerous skirmishes. He was wounded six times, once almost fatally, and had six horses shot from under him.

Gettysburg and Appomattox

Space does not permit a full discussion of the future governor's extraordinary war record. For those unfamiliar with his career, Chamberlain is best remembered for his participation in two dramatic events. The first occurred on July 2, 1863, the second day of the Battle of Gettysburg, and was one of the decisive moments of the war. Colonel Chamberlain made an important decision at a key moment in the battle when he saw the Fifteenth Alabama advancing toward a small hill at the end of the Union line called Little Round Top.

The view from Little Round Top, circa 1895, where the Twentieth Maine, led by Joshua Chamberlain, held off a determined Confederate attack on Little Round Top. *Courtesy of Maine Memory Network.*

As Confederate forces were attempting to take the hill, Chamberlain positioned 386 men from the Twentieth Maine to defend Little Round Top from the assault. As the Alabama soldiers swept up the hill toward Union forces, they collided with Chamberlain's troops in a savage battle.

As Chamberlain later wrote:

> *The flanking column worked around to our left and joined those before us in a fierce assault, which lasted with increasing fury for an intense hour. The two lines met and broke and intermingled in the shock. The crush of musketry gave way to cuts and thrusts, grapplings and wrestlings. The edge of the conflict swayed to and fro. At times I saw before me more of the enemy than of my own men.*

With over 120 casualties and with their ammunition running low, the situation was becoming critical for the Maine soldiers. Seeing signs of exhaustion among the Confederates, Chamberlain rallied his troops, including his two brothers, who were officers in the regiment, and ordered a bayonet charge. "The fighting professor and his Down Easters proved equal to the occasion," wrote Civil War historian James M. McPherson. The Twentieth Maine

On the last day of the Battle of Gettysburg (July 3, 1863), Union forces repulsed the famous Pickett's Charge of advancing Confederates. *Author's collection.*

From Generals to Governors

charged down the hill, capturing 300 Confederates and successfully saving the Union flank. Chamberlain said, "Our left swung first, the advancing foe stopped, tried to make a stand amidst the trees and boulders, but the frenzied bayonets pressing through every space forced a constant settling to the rear."

Chamberlain, who was in the thick of the battle, sustained two wounds, though neither was serious. Many years later, he was awarded the Medal of Honor for "his daring heroism and great tenacity in holding his position on Little Round Top."

The second of the two dramatic events was equally moving, though nonviolent. At the end of the war Chamberlain was with Ulysses S. Grant when Robert E. Lee surrendered at Appomattox Court House in April 1865. He had been promoted to brigadier general in 1864 following what was thought at the time to be a mortal wound during the siege of Petersburg. (Many, including his wife, Fanny, urged him to resign, but he was determined to serve to the end of the war). Subsequently he was brevetted (promoted) to major general by President Lincoln.

At Appomattox, Grant chose Chamberlain to review the parade of Confederate infantry as a part of the formal surrender. As the despondent Southern army advanced, Chamberlain, who was deeply touched by the honor, called his men to attention and saluted the Confederates as they approached. Southern general John Gordon, hearing the shifting of weapons and recognizing the honor, rose in his stirrups and ordered his troops to return the salute. Although the event generated a certain amount of controversy in the North, it helped to begin the postwar healing process.

The grand review, May 23, 1865, where Joshua Chamberlain led his troops in the parade of the Army of the Potomac in Washington, D.C. *Courtesy of Library of Congress, Prints and Photographs Division.*

Governor and Beyond

General Chamberlain found it difficult to adjust to civilian life after the war. His marriage with Fanny had become so strained that the couple separated for a year before patching up their relationship. Chamberlain briefly resumed his professorship at Bowdoin, but he found the academic routine dull and uninspiring. Capitalizing on his immense popularity, the ex-general then decided to pursue a political career and run for governor.

Joshua Chamberlain was elected governor of Maine in 1866, winning 62 percent of the vote, a record at the time. He broke this record the next year, garnering 72 percent of the vote, and again defeated the Democratic candidate, Eben Pillsbury. As a four-term governor, Chamberlain helped to establish a new agricultural and technical college at Orono, which would eventually grow into the University of Maine. With the state's economy in decline after the war, he worked to attract outside investment. To further aid the state's economy, Governor Chamberlain encouraged immigrants, many of whom were from Scandinavia, to become farmers. Throughout this period, Chamberlain continued to live in Brunswick, commuting to Augusta by train as state business required.

Maine was relatively prosperous during Chamberlain's tenure. In fairness, however, it should be mentioned that his four years in office were not entirely free of strife. He enforced such controversial measures as capital punishment, and he generated a certain amount of unrest by refusing to create a special force to enforce the prohibition of alcohol.

After serving the state for four terms, Governor Chamberlain retired and returned to pursue his enduring interest in education. In 1871, the board of trustees appointed him the sixth president of Bowdoin College, where he remained until ill health forced him to step down in 1883. Chamberlain restructured the college curriculum and introduced courses in science and engineering, practically unheard of at the time. At the same time, he continued to write, teach and take lecture tours around the country and Europe.

The new president's wartime experiences had accustomed him to giving orders and seeing them obeyed. This particular trait, however, was less suitable when dealing with college students. When regular military drill, in uniform, was introduced as a part of the curriculum, the student body was only mildly enthusiastic. This turned to open hostility in the "Drill Rebellion of 1874," when students saw it as an attempt to turn Bowdoin into a military school. Drill was dropped from the curriculum when Chamberlain lost the support of the board of trustees.

From Generals to Governors

Leaving Bowdoin in 1883, the former governor pursued various activities during the last thirty years of his life. This included everything from land speculation in Florida to writing about education, Maine and his Civil War memoir, *The Passing of the Armies*. Chamberlain was an active member of the Grand Army of the Republic, and he was considered one of the great orators of his day. Not surprisingly, he was in constant demand as a speaker at soldiers' reunions.

Chamberlain never really recovered from the near-fatal wound he had received in his hip and groin at Petersburg in 1864. Six operations were unable to cure the pain and infections that constantly plagued him. In addition, he was forced to wear a primitive form of catheter the rest of his life.

By 1898, his life began to slow down. The seventy-year-old general volunteered for duty in the Spanish-American War, but to his great disappointment, he was rejected. He was briefly reenergized in 1900 when he was named surveyor of the Port of Portland, but in 1905, Fanny died, following complications from a broken hip. Sadly, her husband did not arrive home until after her death.

In May 1913, Chamberlain was planning the fiftieth anniversary of the Battle of Gettysburg, but he was unable to attend the ceremonies due to deteriorating health. Joshua Lawrence Chamberlain, "One of the Knightliest Soldiers," according to Confederate general John Gordon at Appomattox, died early the next year at the age of eighty-five.

THE THIRTY-FIFTH GOVERNOR: SELDON CONNOR

He was present at the first Civil War battle, where he fought as a private. Three years later, he had risen to the rank of brigadier general and had survived some of the bloodiest conflicts in the war, until he was seriously wounded in the Battle of the Wilderness. It is not an overstatement to say that Seldon Connor's military career compares favorably to any of Maine's Civil War heroes, saving that of Joshua Chamberlain.

The future general and governor was born in 1839 and was educated in local public schools in Fairfield, Maine, a few miles west of Augusta. Connor graduated from Tufts College at the age of twenty in 1859. After graduation, he moved to Woodstock, Vermont, and began to read law at the offices of Washburn and Marsh.

When the Civil War broke out, President Lincoln issued a call for 75,000 volunteers to combat the rebellion. Connor responded by enlisting for three

Seldon Connor entered the army as a private and rose to the rank of brigadier general in the Union army.
Courtesy of Library of Congress, Prints and Photographs Division.

months in a local regiment, the First Vermont Infantry volunteers. On June 10, 1861, his Vermont unit was engaged in the first major action of the war, the Battle of Bethel Church, which is on the tip of the Yorktown peninsula. Unfortunately for Connor and his Vermont comrades, the battle resulted in a Southern victory, when a Confederate force of 1,500 men routed a disorganized Union army of 3,500.

Connor's three-month tour of duty ended in August. He returned to Maine and joined the Seventh Maine volunteers with the rank of lieutenant colonel, presumably because of his prior military experience. Connor's new regiment saw their first action the following year in the Peninsula Campaign. He was then appointed commander of the Nineteenth Maine Regiment, which saw action in the battles of Antietam, Fredericksburg and Gettysburg.

On May 6, 1864, Connor, by now a brigade commander and a full colonel, was badly wounded in the Battle of the Wilderness. At a critical moment in the battle, his brigade came to the aid of General Winfield Scott Hancock's Second Corps that had been routed by Confederate general James Longstreet's attack. During the course of the melee, a musket ball shattered Connor's left thighbone. For his gallant service, President Lincoln promoted the twenty-five-year-old Connor to the rank of brigadier general.

The wound put Connor out of commission for the remainder of the war. He spent a year convalescing in a Washington hospital before he was sent back to his family home in Fairfield, still immobilized. In the spring of 1866, in constant pain from the imperfectly knit bones in his leg, Connor fell and fractured the same leg. He was confined to his house for two more years.

From Generals to Governors

Connor was severely wounded in the bloody Battle of the Wilderness in 1864. *Courtesy of Print and Picture Collection, Free Library of Philadelphia.*

Parts of the Wilderness Battlefield today are still a tangle of woods and streams. *Author's collection.*

During his Washington hospitalization, Connor met Henrietta "Nettie" Bailey, whose family lived in the area. The story is that Nettie was visiting wounded soldiers when she met Seldon, and they fell in love. After a courtship of several years, they were married in October 1869. The enamored Connor wrote to Nettie shortly before they married: "In less than a week, beloved, I shall be heart to heart with the most beautiful, the sweetest and dearest love since the world began…It gives me great joy to read the words that tell me you are mine and will go with me wherever I go."

General Connor's political career began in 1868 as a member of Governor Chamberlain's staff. This was followed by his appointment to the post of assessor of internal revenue for the Third District of Maine. When the office was abolished, he became collector of internal revenue for the Augusta area.

Connor held this position until he was nominated by the Republican Party to run for governor. In 1875, he was elected Maine's thirty-fifth governor by a sizable majority over the Democratic candidate, Charles Roberts. This was followed by his reelection in 1876 and 1877. During his three terms, Governor Connor was a strong advocate for civil service reform as well as public schooling for all citizens. He was also a forceful proponent of the prohibition of alcohol as well as the elimination of land grants to railroads. The following excerpt is from his message to the legislature in 1876 regarding liquor: "Maine has a fixed conclusion upon this subject. It is that the sale of intoxicating liquors is an evil of such magnitude that the wellbeing of the state demands, and the condition of social compact warrants, its suppression."

In 1878, Connor, seeking a fourth term, lost a disputed election to Alonzo Garcelon, the Democratic candidate. Maine's constitution at the time required the winner to receive a majority of the votes. Connor had won 44 percent; Garcelon, 22 percent; and the Greenback Party candidate, John Smith, 34 percent. The election was thus thrown into the state legislature, where Garcelon and Smith joined forces to defeat Connor. (The state constitution has since been amended so that a plurality is sufficient to elect).

Connor's career, however, was far from over. In 1882, President Chester Arthur appointed him United States pension agent for the State of Maine, an office he held until 1887. He spent the next four years as president of the Northern Banking Company in Portland. Then, in 1892, Governor Henry Cleaves appointed him adjutant general of Maine. That same year he was also offered the presidency of Maine State College, the future University of Maine. Despite heavy pressure from the college, he declined the offer, apparently for financial reasons.

Connor remained an important figure in veteran's affairs for the rest of his life. He was a commander of the Grand Army of the Republic, and in 1889, he was chosen to deliver the oration at the dedication of Maine's monuments at the Gettysburg battlefield. It was reported: "Ex-Governor Connor graphically described the part taken in the battle by the various regiments from Maine." The following year he was elected president of the Society of the Army of the Potomac.

In 1897, Connor was reappointed to the position of state pension agent by President William McKinley. Simultaneously, and for the rest of his life, he continued to play a prominent role in the state's political affairs. When Brigadier General Seldon Connor died in 1917 at the age of seventy-eight, he was one of nine remaining Union officers of that rank.

THE THIRTY-EIGHTH GOVERNOR: HARRIS M. PLAISTED

Harris Plaisted commanded a Union brigade in the Civil War and was, like Joshua Chamberlain and Seldon Connor, a war hero who became a governor. As governor, Plaisted championed the interests of the working class against the business establishment. He so aggravated his opponents that one rival accused him of being a communist.

Although he was born in New Hampshire, Plaisted's Maine roots ran deep. Three of his ancestors, Captain Roger Plaisted and his two sons, were killed in King Philip's War in 1675. The future governor was one of nine children and grew up working on the family farm. His parents were not well off, and their children learned the importance of hard work and piety from an early age.

Plaisted received his formal education at Waterville (now Colby) College, where he graduated in 1853. It is interesting that he was able to pay his tuition by serving as superintendent of schools for Waterville, an elected position. After graduation, Plaisted studied law at the Albany (New York) Law School, where he graduated with highest honors. In 1856, he moved to Bangor and was admitted to the bar.

Married and with a growing family, Plaisted opened a successful law practice in Bangor. When the Civil War broke out, Plaisted was appointed a lieutenant colonel by the governor and directed to form his own company, which he did in thirty days. As commander of the Eleventh Maine Volunteer Regiment, Plaisted successfully led his troops through the series of battles known as the Peninsula Campaign in 1862. The following year he and his men were involved in the siege of Charleston. It was here that his regiment used one of the most famous siege guns in the war, the Swamp Angel, which reportedly could fire a three-hundred-pound shell 3,500 yards with devastating effect.

In 1864, Colonel Plaisted was transferred to the Richmond-Petersburg sector of the eastern front. His troops, dubbed the "Iron Brigade," saw continuous action for two months, losing 1,385 out of 2,698 men. Plaisted performed heroically throughout the campaign. His immediate superior wrote, "The discipline of his brigade is of the highest order, and its fighting qualities unsurpassed by any in the army." Plaisted was twice decorated by President Lincoln and promoted to major general "for gallant and meritorious conduct in the field."

Plaisted was also a very popular leader, as shown by the following resolution that was forwarded to him in Maine from his troops:

> *Resolved. That the unvarying and remarkable successes of his command are the best evidences of General Plaisted's faithfulness and ability as a soldier...he was a worthy commander of the Iron Brigade and we shall ever cherish pleasing recollections of General Plaisted as an able commander, a gallant soldier and an estimable Christian gentleman.*

Richmond and Petersburg took a terrific pounding from Union artillery during a nine-month siege in 1865 and 1865. General Plaistead's Iron Brigade saw continual action. *Courtesy of Print and Picture Collection, Free Library of Philadelphia.*

From Generals to Governors

Back in Bangor after the war, Plaisted resumed his law practice and soon was recognized as one of the best lawyers in the state. Politics beckoned, however, and during the next ten years he was elected to the state legislature twice and as state attorney general three times. As attorney general, he compiled an impressive record, including the successful prosecution of twelve murder cases.

In 1875, Governor Nelson Dingley appointed Plaisted to fill the seat in the Forty-fourth Congress, left open by the death of Representative Samuel Hersey. Congressman Plaisted quickly became an active member of the House. Of special note was his work on Proctor Knott's committee investigating the Whiskey Ring, which was a conspiracy of distillers and government officials attempting to defraud the government. Since President Ulysses S. Grant's private secretary, General Orville E. Babcock, was involved, the committee sought to implicate Grant in the scheme.

After lengthy hearings, Plaisted, the only Republican on the committee, was able to establish that Grant had been the first to discover the frauds and demand that the guilty be punished. Eventually the president was completely vindicated, although his administration continued to be tarnished by scandals. The appreciative Grant offered General Plaisted chief judgeships in Washington and Wyoming, which he declined, preferring to return to Maine.

In 1878, Plaisted chose not to run for Congress. He had become disillusioned with Republican Party politics, and in 1879, he joined the Democratic Party. The next year, the Democrats and the Greenback Party nominated him for governor and, in an extremely close election, he won by barely 200 votes, 73,770–73,544. Plaisted served a term of two years from 1881 to 1883. (Remember, as pointed out in an earlier part of this book, the governor's term was expanded to two years in 1879.)

In 1992, John Hale, a *Bangor Daily News* reporter, wrote an article about Plaisted entitled, "The Maverick Governor from Bangor."

> *The city of Bangor has produced seven of Maine's governors, including the only governor ever elected under the banner of the Fusion Party. His rebel-style politics are a 100-year-old precursor to the modern campaigns of the late James B. Longley (an Independent who was Governor of Maine) and Ross Perot.*

Plaisted's tenure as governor was marked by constant conflicts with the Republicans over the question of political appointments. John Hale said his term could be summed up in one word: "stalemate." While serving as governor, Plaisted further infuriated the Republican Party by championing

Harris Plaistead was the thirty-eighth governor of Maine. His term was marked by frequent conflicts with the Republican Party. *Courtesy of Maine Memory Network.*

the interests of the working class against the business establishment. He was against big corporations and attempted to regulate the railroads, a direct challenge to big business.

James G. Blaine, editor of the *Kennebec Journal* and a future three-term speaker of the House of Representatives, was a strong opponent of Plaisted. In one of his editorials, Blaine wrote, "If carried to their full logical extent, they would go to the farthest limit of the worst kind of communism."

Frederick Robie, Republican candidate for governor, defeated Plaisted in 1883, effectively ending his political career. Following an unsuccessful run for the Senate that same year, he became editor and publisher of the *New Age*, an Augusta newspaper, where he continued to exchange attacks with Blaine.

Governor Harris Plaisted died in 1898 at the age of sixty-nine from Bright's disease (kidney failure), which stemmed from malaria that he contracted while in the army. His portrait hangs in the Statehouse near a picture of his son, Frederick Plaisted, who was the Democratic governor of Maine from 1911 to 1913.

Chapter 3

Soldiers, Sailors and Marines

Generals in Blue:
Rufus Ingalls and Oliver O. Howard

Rufus Ingalls

Rufus Ingalls was born in Denmark, Maine. At West Point he was the roommate of Civil War hero and eighteenth president Ulysses S. Grant, with whom he had a lifelong friendship. As a young lieutenant, Ingalls fought in the Mexican War, distinguishing himself in an engagement near Taos, New Mexico. Rufus Ingalls is best known, however, as an exceptional army quartermaster. Indeed, in 1987, he was the fifth man to be inducted into the Quartermaster Hall of Fame at Fort Lee, Virginia.

Ingalls was the son of a prosperous businessman who was a member of Maine's Constitutional Convention in 1819. Through his father's political connections, he was appointed to West Point, graduating in 1843. The West Point class of 1915 has been called "the class that the stars shined on," since one-third of their graduates became generals, including Dwight Eisenhower and Omar Bradley. The record of Ingalls' class, however, was even more impressive. Sixteen of the thirty-nine members, or 41 percent of the class, went on to become generals.

It is important to understand the duties of a quartermaster. Throughout history, from Alexander the Great to Napoleon, it was impossible for an army to function without effective logistical support. In the Civil War, quartermasters were the "behind the scenes" administrators. They were in charge of supplying the army with its every need. They procured the food,

Rufus Ingalls was one of the outstanding quartermasters in the history of the United States Army. *Courtesy of Library of Congress, Prints and Photographs Division.*

the clothing, the horses, the weapons and ammunition and all manner of camp equipment. They maintained the roads, they built (and rebuilt) railroads and bridges and they maintained the supply depots and paid the bills.

Ingalls's quartermaster career began in 1848, at the start of the California gold rush. His duties on the West Coast took him from Los Angeles to Monterey to Fort Vancouver, in the recently acquired Oregon Territory. In Oregon, Ingalls spent much of his time rafting logs down the Columbia River and supervising the building of Fort Vancouver. At one point during construction, Ingalls ran into his former roommate, Ulysses Grant, who was also in the quartermaster corps. One night the two friends came up with an idea to supplement their meager military salaries. Their plan was to plant one hundred acres of potatoes on the banks of the Columbia. Alas, a flash flood washed away their potato crop as well as their dreams of financial gain.

A few years later, the two classmates teamed up again. This time they planned a scheme to profit from the high prices being charged for ice in San Francisco. The two quartermasters, now captains, arranged to have ice cut in the Fort Vancouver area and shipped to San Francisco. One again nature intervened when headwinds prevented their chartered vessel from reaching port before the cargo of ice had melted. This was enough for Grant, who had a growing family to support. He resigned his commission and returned to Illinois where he continued his struggles to earn a living until the Civil War broke out.

In 1854 the signature event in Ingalls's pre–Civil War career occurred when he accompanied Colonel Edward Steptoe on an expedition from Fort Leavenworth, Kansas, to the Pacific coast. Ingalls was chosen for the mission because, in the words of then secretary of war Jefferson Davis, "he had served with the dragoons (mounted infantry) and had much experience in frontier service." Captain Ingalls was in charge of 175 dragoons, who were to guide 150 settlers and one thousand horses on their journey to California.

In Utah, the expedition stopped to investigate the Gunnison Massacre, which occurred when Pahvant Indians killed John Gunnison and seven members of his Pacific Railroad survey crew. The reasons for the attack are complex, though it may have been in retaliation for the death of a Pahvant chief. Steptoe and Ingalls spent the winter of 1854–1855 investigating the murders before moving on.

Meanwhile, the company had made their winter quarters in the Rush Valley, south of Salt Lake City, where Ingalls constructed two large adobe buildings for winter storage of forage and supplies. When they departed, Ingalls sent a report to the quartermaster general, summarizing what he had done and recommending that the government maintain a facility at Rush Lake because of its suitability as a "reserve." He and Colonel Steptoe also recommended that Brigham Young remain as governor of the Utah Territory.

Civil War Quartermaster

At the start of the Civil War, Ingalls, who by now had gained a reputation as a superb quartermaster, was ordered to Washington to organize the supply system for the Army of the Potomac. He became the chief quartermaster for a succession of Union generals, the first being George B. McClellan, commander of the Peninsula Campaign. After McClellan, Ingalls would demonstrate his logistical skills to Generals Burnside, Hooker and Meade before finally working for his old friend, Ulysses Grant.

Ingalls faced massive challenges in organizing and managing the vast network that supplied the many campaigns conducted by the Army of the Potomac in northern Virginia. Despite frequent changes in Union high command, Ingalls remained that army's chief quartermaster throughout the war. Ingalls's letter to General Meigs on September 28, 1863, indicates the kind of logistical challenges he dealt with on a weekly basis.

> *Our wagon trains had been much increased. About the first of November they numbered 3,911 wagons, 8,693 horses, 12,483 mules, 907 ambulances, 7,139 artillery horses, and 9,582 cavalry. We had sufficient* [material] *to haul seven days supplies for the army, besides its baggage camp and equipage. The army crossed the Potomac on pontoon bridges at Berlin the last* [day] *of October.*

Left: Ulysses S. Grant was a West Point classmate and a lifelong friend of Ingalls. *Author's collection.*

Below: The Beanpole and Cornstalk railroad bridge was named by President Lincoln, who was amazed at its slim structure. It was built over the Potomac Creek in Northern Virginia and was a fine example of Union military engineering. *Courtesy of Print and Picture Collection, Free Library of Philadelphia.*

Soldiers, Sailors and Marines

The Dictator was a seventeen-thousand-pound mortar that Rufus Ingalls had transported on a specially constructed railroad for the siege of Petersburg in 1864. *Author's collection.*

The highpoint of Ingalls's military career was fast approaching. In March 1864, President Lincoln appointed Ulysses S. Grant commander in chief of all Union armies, thus again uniting Ingalls and Grant. A few months later, in an effort to capture Richmond, Grant laid siege to nearby Petersburg, a crucial Confederate rail center. This necessitated the construction of a vast supply depot at City Point, twenty miles south of Richmond on the James River. Ingalls's job was to support Grant's plans for the siege, which would run for the next nine months.

City Point became one of the busiest ports in the world as Ingalls, now brevetted to brigadier general, created a supply depot previously unparalleled in military history. At any one time there were 150 to 200 ships anchored off City Point waiting to unload their cargo.

The expanded port facilities permitted cargo to be loaded straight from ships to either railcars or wagons. In his article, "City Point: The Tool that Gave General Grant Victory," Captain Robert Zinnen elaborates on Ingalls's logistical feat of supporting an army of 500,000 soldiers:

> *The port facilities consisted of eight wharves covering over eight acres with warehouses totaling over 100,000 square feet of the wharves. An intricate rail network of over 22 miles of track spanned from the wharves to directly behind the Union lines. City Point provided rations support to the Union Army such as fresh meat and over 100,000 loaves of fresh bread daily. The massive repair shop located at City Point maintained the force of*

Left: City Point, Virginia, was the chief Union supply base for the siege of Petersburg and Richmond. Coehorn mortars are seen in the foreground and Parrott guns are in the background. *Photo by M. Brady, Courtesy of Library of Congress, Prints and Photographs Division.*

Below: City Point was at the juncture of the James and Appomattox Rivers where Rufus Ingalls was responsible for establishing and maintaining a huge supply base. *Courtesy of Library of Congress, Prints and Photographs Division*

over 5,000 wagons and the 60,000 animals necessary to support Grant's army. During the siege of Petersburg, the hospitals built at City Point were capable of treating 15,000 wounded.

On April 2, 1865, the siege was finally lifted when Confederate general Robert E. Lee evacuated the Richmond/Petersburg area. When Lee surrendered to Grant a week later at Appomattox Court House, Rufus Ingalls was among the few present in the room during the negotiations. Ingalls remained at City Point for the next year, gradually closing down the vast facility. He then returned to Washington in July 1866 to await his next assignment.

For the next sixteen years, Ingalls was chief quartermaster of the Division of the Pacific and the Division of the Missouri. In this capacity, he made frequent tours of the land west of the Mississippi River. His recommendations for fortifications, travel routes, supply depots and means of supply were vital for the settlement, growth and security of the country in the decades following the Civil War.

When Ulysses Grant was elected president in 1868, Ingalls stayed at the White House whenever he was passing through Washington. On February 23, 1882, he was named the sixteenth quartermaster general of the army. The next year, after forty years of service, Ingalls retired from the army. He spent the last years of his life in Oregon, before moving to New York City for medical care shortly before his death. Rufus Ingalls died in 1891 at the age of seventy-four and was buried in Arlington National Cemetery.

In a tribute to his old friend, President Grant wrote in his memoirs, "There has been no army in the United States where the duties of Quartermaster have been so well performed." To this, Captain Zinnen added, "Ingalls' leadership (at City Point) provided constant guidance, support and a mixture of stringent control and autonomy for the different departments." And in his book *Generals in Blue*, Ezra Warner wrote, "It might be said of Ingalls that army commanders might come and go, but he went on forever."

Oliver Otis Howard

The career of O.O. Howard has been called "one of the great paradoxes of American military history" by Ezra Warner in his book, *Generals in Blue*. "No officer entrusted with the field direction of troops has ever equaled Howard's record of surviving so many tactical errors of judgment and emerging not only with increased rank, but on one occasion with the thanks of Congress," wrote Warner.

How did Howard's reputation manage to survive a series of tactical defeats during the first three years of war? Why was he rewarded with promotion to brigadier general? Today we might say he had the benefit of a good public relations officer. Historians have been restrained in their assessments of Howard's career. Some have called it "odd," others have said he benefitted from "fortunate circumstances." The most compelling reason for his survival, however, was that he had the support of President Lincoln.

The son of a farmer, Oliver Howard was born in Leeds, Maine, in 1830. Although his father died when he was nine, Howard was a resourceful young man. He worked his way through Bowdoin, teaching at various grammar schools in the summer. He graduated from the college at the age of nineteen.

Howard was preparing for a teaching career, when he was offered an appointment to West Point by his uncle, Congressman John Otis, which he immediately accepted. Cadet Howard was an excellent student and graduated in 1854, fourth in the class. A distinguished West Point career was marred by a single incident that occurred during his first year, when he "suffered a wound falling out of a tree and landing on his head." This mishap proved to be an omen of things to come, given the wounds and injuries he was to suffer on the battlefield.

In the years before the Civil War, Howard's life was marked by three events. In 1855, he married his longtime sweetheart, Elizabeth Ann Waite from Brunswick, on Valentine's Day. The couple would have seven children. The following year he was sent to Florida to fight in the Seminole Wars. While there, he underwent an intense religious experience and seriously considered resigning from the army to become a minister. His feelings would later earn him the nickname "the Christian General." In 1857, Howard returned to West Point to teach mathematics until the surrender of Fort Sumter, when he joined the Third Maine Volunteers.

At the battle of First Manassas (Bull Run), Colonel O.O. Howard led a brigade of Maine infantry into combat. Although his command was driven from the field, along with the rest of the Union army, Howard was promoted two months later to brigadier general. Following this, the new general suffered the ignominy of falling from a limber (an artillery wagon), which crushed his big toe.

No one would ever question the courage of this "monogamous, tee totaling, Congregationalist," which is what historian James M. McPherson called him. In June 1862, while commanding a Union brigade at the Battle of Fair Oaks, General Howard's right arm was shattered during a charge and had to be amputated. (He would subsequently be awarded the Medal of Honor for his heroism.) When General Philip Kearny, who had lost his left arm, visited him, he quipped that they would "now be able to shop for gloves together."

The undaunted Howard was back from convalescence within three months and saw action at the Battle of Antietam. Unfortunately, his brigade was ambushed and subsequently annihilated by a Confederate force in a matter of minutes. This was followed by the Union disaster at the Battle of Fredericksburg in December 1862. Howard, now brevetted to major general (a temporary battlefield promotion), saw his division routed in the bloody assault on Marye's Heights.

General Oliver Howard was a brave but controversial Union general. *Courtesy of Library of Congress, Prints and Photographs Division.*

General Howard's military career continued to falter at the Battles of Chancellorsville and Gettysburg. At Chancellorsville, he failed to follow Union general Joseph Hooker's orders to protect his right flank. His corps was routed, and he was wounded again by Stonewall Jackson's surprise attack. Although there were calls for Howard's replacement, he had a staunch supporter in Abraham Lincoln, who patiently told critics, "give him time, he will bring things straight."

At Gettysburg, Civil War historian Ezra Warner wrote, "He displayed a conspicuous lack of decision." At a critical point on the first day of the battle, Howard got into a shouting match with Winfield Scott Hancock over seniority until orders arrived from General George Meade, placing Hancock in command. Howard's principal contribution at Gettysburg was that he placed his corps in an important reserve position on Cemetery Hill at a critical period in the battle. Terry Jones, in *Historical Dictionary of the Civil War*, adds: "Although his actions at Gettysburg were not brilliant [his Eleventh

Many historians feel that Howard's military career continued to prosper because he had the support of President Abraham Lincoln. *Author's collection.*

Corps lost three thousand men], Howard received the Thanks of Congress for holding that crucial high ground."

The thirty-two-year-old O.O. Howard may have received the "Thanks of Congress" for his efforts at Gettysburg, but thus far his military career had not been much of a success. Despite the fact that he had lost an arm in battle, Major Thomas Osborne, his chief artillery officer, wrote: "He was not a man gifted with obvious leadership qualities. He was neither a profound thinker nor an officer with large natural ability. Slightly built, 5'9," and pale, he did not call out from the troops enthusiastic applause."

Another of his officers, Captain Winkler wrote, "Most of his strengths were interior ones. He possessed a strong religious conviction that suffused his whole life," hence his moniker, "the Christian General."

In the fall of 1863, General Howard's fortunes finally began to improve. He was transferred to the western theater (Tennessee) and took part in the siege of Chattanooga. Howard's Eleventh Corps was part of the Union assault that drove Confederates from Missionary Ridge and Lookout Mountain, overlooking the city. The next year, following the death of General James McPherson, Howard was given command of the Army of Tennessee.

In the siege of Atlanta, Howard was wounded a third time in a bloody encounter west of the city at Pickett's Mill. A few weeks later, as Union forces closed in on Atlanta, his forces drove Confederates from the field at the Battle of Ezra Church. At the end of the fight, General Howard was cited for "gallant and meritorious service." Following the surrender of Atlanta, Howard commanded the right wing of William Tecumseh Sherman's army in the famous March to the Sea.

Soldiers, Sailors and Marines

The Freedmen's Bureau and Howard University

Howard's military career did not end with the defeat of the Confederacy. (He stayed in the army for over half a century because he needed the money.) One could argue that Howard achieved greater prominence in the postwar years because of his abhorrence of slavery. This would lead to his next position.

Following the death of Abraham Lincoln, President Andrew Johnson, on the advice of General Grant, somewhat reluctantly appointed the zealous Howard to head the Bureau of Refugees, Freedmen and Abandoned Lands. The organization subsequently came to be known as the Freedmen's Bureau. Howard had become deeply concerned with the welfare of the four million former slaves.

> *I could never conceive how a man could become a better laborer by being made to carry an over heavy and wearisome burden which in no way facilitates his work. I could never detect the shadow of a reason why the color of the skin should impair the right to life, liberty and the pursuit of happiness.*

The United States Army ran the Freedmen's Bureau, and its employees were officers. (Today it would be run by the Department of Health and Human Services and the Department of Education.) In his capacity as director, Howard worked valiantly to assist the millions of recently freed African Americans adjust to their new lives. Almost immediately, however, he ran into opposition from the president. Andrew Johnson, a Democrat from Tennessee, was adamantly against the idea that the two races were equal. In fact, no sooner was Howard installed in his post when Johnson began trying to dismantle the bureau and undermine its mission to improve the lot of African Americans.

Realizing that his time was limited, Howard gave top priority to education. "The slaves are becoming free; give them knowledge, teach them to read, teach the child," he wrote. With this in mind, he began to organize schools across the South and cofounded a university in Washington, D.C., that would supply the African American community with teachers, doctors, lawyers and ministers. In 1869, the institution was named Howard University, and Oliver Howard served as its first president from 1869 to 1874.

Otherwise, Howard was not well suited to run the Freedmen's Bureau. He was a poor administrator and spent too much time on the road,

Rations are issued to the old and the sick at the Freedmen's Bureau. Following the war, the bureau's main role was providing emergency food, housing and medical aid to former slaves and helping reunite families. *Courtesy of Library of Congress, Prints and Photographs Division.*

leaving his subordinates unsupervised. The result was that the bureau was plagued by fraud, corruption and inefficiency. In 1872, when Howard returned from one of his trips, he found that Congress had closed down the Freedmen's Bureau.

In 1874, General Howard took his family, his idealism and his evangelism to the West Coast, where he commanded the army's Department of the Columbia for the remainder of the decade. Wherever he went, he preached temperance, racial tolerance and religion. He negotiated a treaty with the Apache leader Cochise, who ended his warring against settlers. He sympathized with the plight of the Nez Perce, who were evicted from their homeland, although ultimately he was forced to use troops against a band of renegades led by Chief Joseph.

Back on the East Coast in 1880, O.O. Howard served as superintendent of West Point until 1882. His next post was commander of the Department of the Platte. Promoted to major general in 1886, his final command was the Department of the East, until he retired in 1894.

Howard stayed active as a writer, speaker and fundraiser for his many causes. He continued his commitment to education, and in 1895, he founded Lincoln Memorial University in Harrogate, Tennessee, for "the education of "mountain whites." Oliver Howard died in Burlington, Vermont, in 1909 at the age of seventy-nine. An impressive equestrian statue of the paradoxical general from Maine stands atop Cemetery Hill on the Gettysburg battlefield.

The "Prohibition Regiment" and General Neal Dow

From the perspective of the twenty-first century, it may be difficult to understand the views of nineteenth-century temperance activist Neal Dow. Well before the Civil War, Dow had become an internationally known figure, famous for his outspoken comments on the evils of alcohol. To understand Dow's position, it is important to place him in the context of his times.

Neal Dow was born in Portland in 1804, the son of a prosperous Quaker businessman. He received a good education at various Portland schools and the Friends Academy in New Bedford, Rhode Island. His formal education ended at the age of sixteen, however, and he went to work in his father's tannery business. In his *Reminiscences*, Dow described the situation: "I much desired to go to college, but my parents were strongly opposed, and I was constrained to conform to their wishes. Their opposition was partially due to the dread of the bad influence upon me of associations that I might form while absent from home."

The "bad influence" he was referring to was undoubtedly the temptations of alcohol. From an early age, Dow was made aware of the problems caused by drink. "I saw health impaired, capacity undermined, employment lost. I saw wives and children suffering from the drinking habits of husbands and fathers." In Dow's youth, Portland was the gateway for the rum trade from the West Indies, and as a conscientious Quaker, Dow was concerned about its effects on people of all classes. As he wrote:

> *Among the rich, educated and refined of the day, frequent victims of intemperance were to be found, as well as among those whose temptation and liability to excess are generally regarded as greater. Liquor found place on all occasions: town meetings, musters, firemen's parades, cattle-shows and fairs. Private assemblies were little better. Weddings, balls, barn raisings, huskings, even funerals were dependent upon intoxicants.*

When he was a young man, Dow began to make speeches around the state in an attempt to educate the public about the problems caused by "strong drink." It was a slow process, and at times he despaired. "At the time of the admission of Maine to the Union (1820) and for thirty years thereafter, her people probably consumed more intoxicating liquor in proportion to their numbers than any other state," he wrote. He cited statistics: "In 1850 not a savings bank existed in Maine." Dow tried to use moral suasion, he tried using religion and then he tried politics.

In 1828, the soon-to-be-married Dow made his first political speech and cast his first presidential vote. Both were for John Quincy Adams, who lost the election to Andrew Jackson. Dow detested Jackson. "His face is employed as a sign for almost all taverns," he wrote to a friend. The country was changing, and Dow began to take an active part in state affairs. He became friends with Hannibal Hamlin, a rising star in Maine politics, and he was a founding member of the Maine Temperance Society.

In 1851, after several unsuccessful attempts, Dow was elected mayor of Portland, on the temperance ticket. The new mayor quickly drafted a law "for the suppression of drinking houses and tippling shops" in the city. He then submitted it to the state legislature. To the astonishment of all, it

The Dow House on Congress Street in Portland, Maine, is open to the public. *Author's collection.*

passed both chambers and was signed into law on June 2, 1851, by Governor John Hubbard. The bill was known nationally as the Maine Law and led to campaigns around the country for prohibition. Neal Dow became a national figure, known as the "Napoleon of Temperance."

Dow lost his bid for reelection when the opposition went to great lengths to defeat him by bringing in hundreds of recently naturalized citizens from Boston to vote on Election Day. As he wrote in his memoirs, "It is easy to understand that Prohibition in Maine was not accepted in a spasm of excitement." Far from discouraged, however, Dow used the opportunity to go on a series of speaking tours around the United States and Canada on behalf of prohibition. He paid his own expenses, although he also raised a lot of money for his cause.

In 1855, running as a member of the newly formed Republican Party, Dow was reelected mayor by 46 votes out of 3,750 cast. In June 1855, the anti-Prohibition forces in Portland instigated what came to be known as the Portland Rum Riot. A man was killed and seven were wounded when Dow ordered police to fire on the mob. The Maine Law was upheld, but Mayor Dow's reputation suffered a setback. Dow accused his opponents of recruiting sailors from boats in the harbor to assist "local roughs in the projected disturbance."

Wartime Experiences

When the Civil War broke out, the fifty-seven-year-old Dow, an ardent opponent of slavery, volunteered his services. Incidentally, he had already been "dismissed from the Society of Friends for differing from it in my views as to war." In the fall of 1861, Maine's governor, Israel Washburn, "addressed me as 'Colonel' and desired me to raise a regiment." Dow agreed but made it clear that he only wanted officers "whose character, tastes and habits were such as would contribute to the morals of those who were to be in my command." And so the Prohibition Regiment was born.

Dow was appointed colonel of the Thirteenth Maine Infantry Regiment. In his *Reminiscences* he describes the enlistment process.

> *Nearly 2,000 men responded to my call and the subscription of the regiment ran over. It had a surplus of 600, which was turned over to other regiments. It reported to be the most temperate and moral of all regiments raised in the state...Among the most pleasing to me were letters received from women saying they were willing for their sons to serve under my command because the influences would be good.*

Although Colonel Dow made his men "take the pledge," there were reports that during training some of them would sneak across the Kennebec River to the grog shops in Augusta when the river froze. Most apparently behaved themselves, and when the Thirteenth broke camp and headed south, Dow could boast that "not one of his men had been arrested for drunkenness." (I should add that this statement from his memoirs has not been verified.)

Dow's wife, Marie, and five children accompanied the regiment to Boston where he bid them farewell. He would not see them for two years. The regiment's voyage south from Boston to the Gulf of Mexico was a traumatic experience. Hundreds of men were "packed like sardines" into the steamer *Mississippi* that had never even taken a trial run. When a bad storm blew up, the ship barely remained afloat.

Brigadier General Neal Dow. The prohibitionist general boasted that, during their training, none of his men were arrested for drunkenness. *Courtesy of Neal Dow Memorial, Portland, Maine*

> *No description can picture the fury of the storm. Water poured into the ship from the deck and through the skylights. At one time the water threatened to extinguish the engine fires. The scene was indescribable in the soldiers' apartments. Some were praying some were cursing, and all were in the most awful suspense. During most of the gale the ship was manned by a man, detached from the Thirteenth Maine, a Portland boy, who stood at the wheel for nine hours.*

After a perilous voyage, which included running aground off the North Carolina coast, the beleaguered *Mississippi* finally arrived at Ship Island, a Union base off of the Mississippi and Louisiana coasts. Promoted to brigadier general, Dow's commands for the next year included the army base on Ship Island, Forts Jackson and St. Philip below New Orleans and the District of West Florida, headquartered at Pensacola. General Dow appears to have been a conscientious commander. The Thirteenth Maine was noted for the perfection of its drill, the thoroughness of its discipline, the cleanliness of its camp and the excellent morale of its men. To this Dow added, "There was, to my knowledge, no drunkenness in my regiment."

In May 1863, the Thirteenth Maine joined a major Union offensive against Port Hudson, a key Confederate fort on the lower Mississippi River. In an assault on the fort on May 27, Dow was wounded twice. "I was struck by a spent ball in my right arm, which was rendered useless and immediately swelled to nearly twice its normal size. Not long after this I was disabled by a rifle ball, which passed through my left thigh above the knee, and I was then helped to the rear."

The campaign against Port Hudson was an important event in the Civil War. About 40,000 Union troops attacked 7,500 Confederate defenders, which resulted in a forty-eight-day siege in the summer of 1863. It is significant that, during the battle, African American troops were used by the North and fought bravely. On July 9, 1863, after hearing that nearby Vicksburg had fallen, Port Hudson surrendered. This gave the Union control of the Mississippi River, which essentially split the Confederacy.

Meanwhile, the wounded General Dow had been transported to the plantation of a Mrs. Cage. General William Tecumseh Sherman sent the convalescing Dow an encouraging message. "You are now at an age where an occasional glass will do you good." (Dow does not appear to have been amused). A few weeks later, Dow's hostess, Mrs. Cage, tipped off a passing squad of Confederate cavalry about her famous patient. On the evening of June 30, 1863, General Dow was captured and taken by wagon, first to Mobile and then to the infamous Libby Prison in Richmond.

As he traveled slowly across the beleaguered South, some of Dow's observations are worth noting.

> *I observed that the Confederate armies were as a mere empty eggshell; there was nothing behind them, the country being drained of its materials and able-bodied men...Our peoples in the North could have but a faint idea of the sacrifices made by the South and the sufferings its people were enduring...every mile I traveled furnished evidence to me of the utter hopelessness of the Southern cause.*

Neal Dow was captured in 1863 and spent eight months in the notorious Libby Prison in Richmond, Virginia. *Courtesy of Neal Dow Memorial, Portland, Maine.*

At the Libby Prison, Dow tried to make the best of the harsh conditions. His age, rank and reputation accorded him better accommodations than most of the prisoners, who "lived in every stage of destitution and misery." In his *Reminiscences*, General Dow states he attempted to raise the morale of his fellow prisoners by giving occasional lectures on the benefits of prohibition and temperance. Not surprisingly, this only antagonized his captors as well as many of his fellow prisoners. "That crank Dow is urging temperance on a lot of men who couldn't get enough to eat to keep them from starving," he reported overhearing from an eavesdropping Confederate officer.

There must have been a sigh of relief from guards and prisoners alike when, on February 25, 1864, General Dow was finally exchanged for Confederate general Fitzhugh Lee, a son of Robert E. Lee. Shortly after his release, Dow resigned from the army and returned to Maine. His health was so broken after eight months in prison that the war was over by the time he recovered his strength.

For the remainder of his life, Neal Dow continued to preach the gospel of temperance throughout the country as well as across the European continent. He cofounded the National Temperance Society and Publishing House to help publicize his cause, and in 1880, he ran unsuccessfully for president on the National Prohibition Party ticket. Dow received 10,305 votes in an election won by James Garfield. In 1884, at the age of eighty, Dow was instrumental in amending Maine's constitution to "prohibit the manufacture or sale of intoxicating beverages."

When Neal Dow died on October 2, 1897, tributes to him poured in from across the state. Perhaps the words of the *Kennebec Journal* summarize his life as well as any. "He would not compromise with the enemy, whether fighting the liquor trade or the foes of the Union."

Unless otherwise noted, the quotations used are taken from The Reminiscences of Neal Dow, *published in 1898.*

THE ADMIRAL: HENRY KNOX THATCHER

It must have been difficult to be the grandson of a Founding Father, especially one as dynamic as Henry Knox, Washington's first secretary of war. The huge (six-foot-two, 280-pound) Knox was larger than life, and he dominated the world of those around him.

His grandson, Henry Knox Thatcher, was born in May 1806 in Thomaston, Maine, just five months before his grandfather died. Young Henry was the second of eight children of Knox's daughter, Lucy, and her husband, Ebenezer Thatcher, a Harvard-educated lawyer. Thatcher would manage the family's affairs after the death of his famous father-in-law.

Their son, Henry, grew up in the family mansion Montpelier, in Thomaston, and from an early age, his head was filled with tales of his grandfather's exploits: how he transported sixty tons of artillery across New England in the dead of winter at the start of the Revolution; how he proposed plans for a federal government that were amazingly prescient in anticipating the U.S. Constitution; and how, as secretary of war, he reorganized the army, created a navy, constructed a system of coastal forts and made a treaty with Indian tribes.

When he moved to Maine as a private citizen in 1794, General Knox's energy was continually on display. He launched ambitious programs in farming, blacksmithing, granite cutting, lumbering, lime burning, salt making, canal building and shipbuilding. The problem was that, after Knox's untimely death in 1806, no associate or family member possessed his energy or vision. Unfortunately, the general's only son, Henry, was irresponsible and unequal to the task of maintaining his father's business enterprises.

Montpelier, the Knox family home in Thomaston, Maine, was where Henry Thatcher grew up and where the presence of his grandfather, Henry Knox, loomed large. *Courtesy of the Collections of Montpelier, the General Henry Knox Museum.*

It is interesting that when Knox's daughter, Lucy, died in 1854, the old general's grandson and future admiral, Henry K. Thatcher, lacked the desire or means to support the decaying old mansion. The property was sold, furnishings auctioned off and, after years of standing vacant, the building was destroyed in 1871.

Henry K. Thatcher was still living in the shadow of Henry Knox when he was admitted to West Point in 1822. Incidentally, the United States Military Academy was another of his grandfather's projects that came to fruition when it was founded in 1802.

Cadet Thatcher stayed only a few months at West Point before he resigned and, following an illness, joined the navy. It must have been a difficult decision for the young man who was trying to decide which career path to take. We are told, however, he "preferred" the navy. He was subsequently appointed an acting midshipman, since the Naval Academy was not founded until 1845. (Before that year, midshipmen were trained by senior officers.) Midshipman Thatcher was then ordered to join a fleet commanded by Commodore David Porter, who was preparing an operation against pirates in the West Indies.

As a member of the United States Navy, Thatcher served on American warships all over the world until the outbreak of the Civil War. He was "passed midshipman" in 1829 and commissioned a lieutenant in 1833. That same year, Thatcher married Susan Croswell of Plymouth, Massachusetts. The couple had no children of their own, although they eventually adopted a niece, the daughter of one of Thatcher's sisters.

Thatcher's first sea command came in 1833, when he was made acting captain of USS *Erie* in the West Indies. From 1839 to 1841, he was attached to USS *Brandywine* in the Mediterranean Squadron. This was followed by a cruise on *Jamestown* from 1847 to 1850, which was part of the African Squadron attempting to suppress the slave trade. Shortly before the Civil War, Thatcher was given command of the sloop of war USS *Decatur* in the Pacific. During his lengthy career, Thatcher made two cruises in the Pacific, two in the West Indies and the Gulf of Mexico and three tours of the Mediterranean. When Thatcher was promoted to commander in 1855, he was "passed-over" eighty-seven senior officers by a special naval selection board.

Admiral Thatcher served all over the world before seeing action in 1864 in the Union attack on Fort Fisher, North Carolina. *Courtesy of the Collections of Montpelier, the General Henry Knox Museum.*

When not on sea duty, Thatcher had a variety of shore duties, chiefly at the Boston and Portland, Maine navy yards. From 1854 to 1855, however, he was executive officer of the Naval Asylum in Philadelphia. The Philadelphia Naval Asylum was a hospital as well as a home for retired sailors. Beginning in 1838, another function of the Naval Asylum was as an academy for aspiring midshipmen, which made it the predecessor of the United States Naval Academy.

From 1859 to the end of 1861, Thatcher was executive officer of the Boston Navy Yard, which meant he was at least partially responsible for the enormous expansion of the navy that took place on the eve of the Civil War. At the end of this assignment, much to his dismay, he was given command of the frigate *Constellation* and assigned to the Mediterranean Squadron. The result was that he was unable to participate in combat operations until the last year of the war.

Nineteenth-century naval historian J.T. Headley has this to say about Thatcher's situation, which was certainly not unique to naval officers in any war:

> *Many of our accomplished commanders had no opportunity of performing any brilliant action, they either being kept on stations at points where it was necessary to have a portion of our navy or where no opportunity occurred of meeting the enemy. Their services, however, were none-the less valuable.*

In Action at Last

Late in the fall of 1864, Thatcher, in the words of J.T. Headley, was able to "show his capacity for commanding a fleet, and conducting active operations." Promoted to commodore, he led the first division of Admiral David Dixon Porter's fleet in a series of attacks on Fort Fisher, which protected the vital

Thatcher was in command of USS *Colorado*, a screw steam frigate, in the attack on Fort Fisher. *Courtesy of Library of Congress, Prints and Photographs Division.*

Soldiers, Sailors and Marines

Confederate port of Wilmington, North Carolina. Wilmington was one of two Southern towns on the Atlantic that remained open, largely due to the presence of Fort Fisher.

In the assault on Fort Fisher, Commodore Thatcher was in command of the steam frigate *Colorado*. In the course of an hour, the ship fired over 1,500 shells at the "Southern Gibraltar," as Fort Fisher was called. Although *Colorado* was seriously hit six times, Thatcher kept his ship in the battle, and according to Headley:

> *He lay abreast of the formidable batteries raining shot and shell on the fortifications. Now, a hundred and fifty pound shot went crashing through his berth deck, soon another tore through his gun deck making an ugly opening. A third pierced the port side of his ship above the water line. But though under such an awful fire and receiving a terrible pounding, Thatcher fought on as coolly as though only testing the range of his guns.*

Fort Fisher was captured on January 15, 1865. In his report of the action, Admiral Porter wrote:

The attack on Fort Fisher as viewed from the land. Union ships are seen in the background.
Courtesy of Library of Congress, Prints and Photographs Division.

First and foremost of the commodores is Commodore H.K. Thatcher. His vessel was always ready for action and was handled with admirable skill. No vessel in the squadron was so cut up as Colorado; *as for some reason the rebels selected her for a target. He has shown the kind of ability naval leaders should possess, a love of fighting and an invincible courage. There is no reward too great for this gallant officer.*

Thatcher's reward for his heroic services was a promotion to rear admiral and orders to take command of the west Gulf Coast squadron, which was blockading Mobile, Alabama. Although Admiral David Farragut had defeated a Confederate fleet at the entrance to Mobile Bay in August 1864, the city had not surrendered to Union forces. Farragut's victory had, however, closed the port to blockade runners.

In cooperation with the Union army, led by General Edward Canby, Rear Admiral Thatcher immediately began operations against Mobile. Suffice to say, the city put up a spirited resistance. Rebel forts lined the vast inner bay, which was still filled with mines, or torpedoes, as they were called at the time. For the next few weeks, and in the face of fierce opposition, Thatcher systematically worked his fleet across Mobile Bay, removing over 150 mines as well as other obstructions from the channel. In the process, he lost six ships and dozens of men while clearing a passage to the city. Mobile finally surrendered on April 12, 1865, three days after the surrender of Robert E. Lee at Appomattox Court House.

Thatcher then moved his squadron to New Orleans, which quickly surrendered. His last stop was Texas, where he took possession of the forts at the mouth of the Sabine River and Galveston, without a fight. In early June, with hostilities finally over, Thatcher was placed in command of the consolidated Gulf Squadron, where he remained for a year.

In 1868, when he reached the age of sixty-two, Henry K. Thatcher was placed on the retired list. Although officially "retired," he served as port admiral of Portsmouth, New Hampshire, until 1871. When he died of kidney disease in 1880, Secretary of the Navy Richard W. Thompson ordered flags to be flown at half-mast and thirteen gun salutes to be fired in his honor.

During Admiral Thatcher's forty-five-year career, the United States Navy emerged as a force in international affairs. Although his participation in combat was limited, Henry Thatcher demonstrated the leadership and courage under fire that won him the admiration of his men and approval of his superiors. His grandfather would have been proud of him.

Soldiers, Sailors and Marines

Two Skippers: The Craven Brothers

One brother received a controversial court-martial at the end of the war; the other went down with his ship at the Battle of Mobile Bay. Thomas Tingey Craven and Tunis Augustus Macdonough Craven were nineteenth-century naval officers and members of a Maine seafaring family that dated back to before the Revolutionary War. Both Craven brothers served with distinction in the Civil War, fighting for the Union. The older brother, Thomas Craven, survived the war and, following his court-martial, was promoted to rear admiral. Tunis Craven died heroically at Mobile Bay in 1864.

Thomas Tingey Craven

Thomas Tingey Craven was born in 1808 in the District of Columbia. He entered the navy as a midshipman in 1822 and was "passed midshipman" in 1828. (The United States Naval Academy was not founded until 1845. Prior to that time young men pursuing a naval career were trained on shipboard and at shore establishments under senior officers.)

Craven saw his first action in 1828 when his ship *Erie* was involved in a fight and subsequent capture of the pirate ship *Federal*. Craven served on various vessels until 1838–1839, when he was appointed first lieutenant on the sloop *Vincennes*, flagship of the United States Exploring Expedition, led by Charles Wilkes that sailed around the world.

In 1841, Craven married Emily Henderson, daughter of the surgeon general of the United States, and built a home for his new family in Kittery Point, Maine. From 1843 to 1844, as captain of the brig USS *Porpoise*, Craven was a member of Commodore Matthew Perry's squadron that patrolled the African coast in an attempt to suppress the slave trade.

In 1850, Craven was made commander of the United States Naval Academy at Annapolis, where he was stationed for most of that decade. He was an innovative leader and instituted a number of curriculum reforms. One was the outfitting, sailing and administration of the ship used for the annual summer practice cruises. Craven commanded the first vessel that took such a cruise, which is still regarded as one of the most beneficial features of the course of study at the naval academy.

Shortly before the outbreak of the Civil War, Craven was assigned to Portland, Maine, where he was put in charge of the navy's recruiting service. When the war broke out, he was promoted to captain and given command of the Potomac Flotilla, guarding Washington, D.C.

Admiral David Farragut was commander of Union naval operations in the Gulf of Mexico. Farragut voted against Thomas Tingey Craven in a controversial court-martial. *Courtesy of Print and Picture Collection, Free Library of Philadelphia.*

In the summer of 1861, Craven was made captain of USS *Brooklyn*, a steam-propelled sloop in the Union's Gulf of Mexico fleet, led by Admiral David Farragut. It is important to note that both Craven brothers would be involved in naval operations that involved Admiral Farragut in the Gulf of Mexico. Each would demonstrate the highest degree of courage and coolness when under fire from Confederate forts and ships.

The older Craven's moment of glory came in April 1862 when Admiral Farragut's fleet, including Craven's USS *Brooklyn*, was ordered to attack Forts Jackson and St. Philip at the entrance to the Mississippi River; the forts had been built to guard New Orleans, the largest city in the Confederacy. When Farragut's flagship, USS *Hartford*, ran hard aground between the forts, it was exposed to intense fire. Craven stopped USS *Brooklyn* and brought her alongside *Hartford*. From this position, he was able to divert enemy fire until Farragut could be "extricated from his perilous position."

His shipmates noted Craven's personal courage during the battle. According to Midshipman John R. Bartlett, "he stood at the forward edge of the deck, his hands on ratlines and did not once move during the action. I have had the good fortune to serve with many brave commanders, but I have never met a man of such consummate coolness, such perfect and apparent indifference to danger as Captain Craven." After the battle, Admiral Farragut exclaimed, "I never saw such rapid and precise firing. It has never been surpassed and probably never was equaled. You and your noble ship have been the salvation of my squadron."

Soldiers, Sailors and Marines

The attack on Fort Jackson, in which Admiral Farragut's ship, USS *Hartford*, was saved by Thomas Tingey Craven's ship, USS *Brooklyn*. *Courtesy of Print and Picture Collection, Free Library of Philadelphia.*

In recognition of his exploits, Thomas Craven was promoted to the rank of commodore in July 1862. Throughout the next year, he served under Farragut in operations along the Mississippi River, climaxing in the siege and capture of Vicksburg in 1863.

Had Commodore Craven died in 1863, he might well be remembered as one of our great naval heroes. Unfortunately, this was not to be. In December of that year, Commodore Craven was directed to take the steam frigate *Niagara* to Europe with orders to protect American commerce against Confederate raiders. In August 1864, he captured the Confederate steamer *Georgia* off the coast of Portugal. Eight months later, off the coast of Spain, he was faced with a crucial decision that would affect his career. The commander of the powerful Confederate ironclad ram *Stonewall* challenged *Niagara* to battle. Realizing his ship was of inferior armament, Craven declined the challenge—a response that would haunt him for years to come.

Mainers in the Civil War

The Court-Martial of Thomas Tingey Craven

After the Civil War, a court-martial was convened to examine the conduct of Commodore Craven versus *Stonewall*. The transcript of the trial is revealing. Every witness called supported Craven's actions as being prudent and even courageous. All agreed that, had he sought battle with *Stonewall*, the result would have been a disaster. At no time during the cross-examination of witnesses was the court able to establish an action by Craven that could be criticized. As a result, the verdict of the court is astonishing—but we are getting ahead of ourselves.

Ironically, the president of the court-martial was Vice-Admiral David Farragut, who one might think would have been favorably disposed toward the accused. Remember, it was Craven who had performed so heroically in saving Farragut's ship USS *Hartford* on the lower Mississippi in 1862.

In a letter to the court, Secretary of the Navy Gideon Welles described the situation in which Craven was charged with "failing to do his utmost to overtake and capture or destroy a vessel which it was his duty to encounter."

> *On the 24th day of March, 1865 the said Commodore Thomas T. Craven, commanding USS* Niagara *and having also under his control the steamer USS* Sacramento, *then lying off Coruna on the coast of Spain, did fail to use any exertions or make any effort to overtake and capture or destroy the vessel,* Stonewall, *as it was his duty to have done; his pretext being that, "the odds in her (the* Stonewall's*) favor were too great.*

The trial ran for sixteen days, and the transcript runs for 173 pages. At issue was the question of whether USS *Niagara*, and her sister ship USS *Sacramento*, should have challenged the *Stonewall*. Craven announced that he would conduct his own defense, assisted by a third brother, Alfred Craven, who was both a lawyer and a civil engineer.

Craven outlined his case in a letter he wrote to Honorable H.J. Perry, Charge d' Affaires, Madrid. In it, he stated "the deep humiliation" he felt that he could not attack *Stonewall*.

> *There she was steaming back and forth flaunting her flags and waiting for me to go out to the attack; I dared not do it, the condition of the sea (no wind) was such that it would have been perfect madness for me to go out. We would have exposed ourselves to almost instant destruction.*

Soldiers, Sailors and Marines

The Confederate ram *Stonewall*, which Thomas Craven refused to engage with his wooden ships, resulting in his court-martial. *Courtesy of Library of Congress, Prints and Photographs Division.*

In a letter to the secretary of the navy, Gideon Welles, Craven reiterated the point. "It may appear that I ought to have run the hazard of a battle, but according to my judgment, I shall ever feel that I have done all that could properly be attempted towards retarding the operations and progress of that vessel."

A partial list of the witnesses' testimony follows:
- Bernard Magill, an ensign on *Niagara*, commented, "*Stonewall* was a very formidable looking vessel." He further supported his view by stating that, in the opinion of an American-born engineer named Palmer, employed by the Spanish navy, "*Stonewall* could easily sink two vessels like *Niagara* and *Sacramento*."
- Eban Hoyt, another lieutenant on *Niagara*, stated, "*Stonewall* would have destroyed *Niagara*, and perhaps both vessels." Hoyt went on to say that, had he been in command, he would have probably engaged *Stonewall* since he would not have had the courage to resist the pressure Craven was under to attack.

- William Roberts, *Niagara*'s chief engineer, stated that *Niagara* had no chance whatsoever to defeat *Stonewall*. "The probabilities were all in favor of the iron-clad sinking the wooden ships."
- William Hitchcock, *Niagara*'s chaplain, referred to Craven as, "a brave and judicious commander, not governed by any unworthy or selfish motives…It took more courage not to attack."

In spite of what appeared to be overwhelming evidence to the contrary, the court found Craven guilty of "defective judgment and a want of zeal and exertion." He was ordered suspended from duty for two years and put on "leave pay." Fortunately for Craven, Secretary of the Navy Gideon Welles reversed the court's verdict, on the grounds that the findings were inconsistent with the evidence presented. Craven was thus "discharged from arrest." The secretary, nevertheless, was of the opinion that "the Commodore was too cautious an officer." (Was this statement issued to appease the court after reversing their verdict?)

Craven's career was not quite over. He was commissioned a rear admiral in 1866 and put in charge of the Navy Yard at Mare Island, California. In 1869, Craven commanded the North Pacific Squadron, and in 1870, he was named port admiral of San Francisco until his retirement in December of that year. Thomas Craven spent the rest of his life at his home in Kittery Point, Maine. He died in 1887 and was buried in Arlington National Cemetery.

The Hero: Tunis Craven

The youngest of the three Craven brothers, Tunis Augustus McDonough Craven, was born in 1813 at the Portsmouth Naval Shipyard in Kittery, Maine. Tunis Craven began his naval career as a midshipman in 1829. He "passed midshipman" in 1835 and was assigned to a number of different ships until 1837. That year, he requested assignment to the United States Coastal Survey Service, where he served for the next decade in a variety of locations and on a variety of vessels. In 1848, as commander of the sloop of war USS *Dale*, he was a member of the Pacific squadron that helped the United States seize California during the Mexican War.

After the war, Lieutenant Craven returned to the East Coast and continued his survey work. In 1854, he and a fellow officer made important observations studying the relationship of bottom topography to the nature of the Gulf Stream current.

In 1857, the navy, recognizing Craven's abilities as a leader and an able surveyor, placed him in command of the Arato Expedition. Since the discovery of gold in California in 1848–1849, the growth of commerce and traffic across the Isthmus of Panama had increased dramatically. For many years, the Arato River region in Nicaragua had been considered as a possible route for a canal across this narrow part of Central America. Craven's charge was to survey the Arato region, which was considered to be an exceedingly difficult project, given the uncharted nature of the area. The expedition encountered many hardships, and the men in the survey team were often on the verge of starvation. Ultimately, however, the mission was successfully completed. With the coming of the Civil War, the project was suspended, so we will never know whether Craven's survey would have been acted upon. When a canal was built across the isthmus forty-five years later, the Arato route was not chosen.

Tunis Craven had a distinguished naval career before the war. *Courtesy of Library of Congress, Prints and Photographs Division.*

Craven's next assignment was equally challenging and probably even more unpleasant. He was put in command of the steam brig *Mohawk*, with orders to patrol the waters of the Caribbean and intercept slave ships coming from Africa. Between 1838 and 1859, United States naval forces had captured only two slavers, since there was little support from the government to restrict the slave trade. The navy's effort to patrol three thousand miles of African coast with three or four ships was virtually impossible.

In 1859, however, President James Buchanan increased naval patrols, and four ships were stationed in the sea around Cuba alone, their purpose being to intercept the illegal American slave ships heading for Southern states. From 1859 to 1860, seven ships were seized, resulting in the liberation of nearly 4,300 Africans. Craven alone apprehended four slavers, including a brig with 500 Africans on board.

Writing to his superiors in Washington, he tried to convey the horrors of the slave trade.

> *The Negroes are packed below in as dense a mass as possible for human beings to be crowded. The space allotted them being in general about four feet height between decks, there of course can be but little ventilation given. These unfortunate creatures are obliged to tend to the calls of nature in this place—tubs being provided for the purpose—and there they pass their days, their nights, amidst the most horrid offensive odors of which the mind can conceive and under the scorching heat of the tropical sun, without room enough for sleep, with scarcely space to die in.*

By this time, Tunis Craven had made quite a name for himself. In 1860, he received a gold medal from Queen Isabella II of Spain for the rescue of the crew of a Spanish merchant ship. Shortly afterward, the United States Board of Underwriters presented his wife with a silver service "for the efficient service rendered to merchant vessels while at sea" by her husband.

Craven was also becoming a determined Unionist, as evidenced by this extract from a letter he wrote to the secretary of the navy, in which he referred to "the present deplorable condition of affairs in the Southern States." With the outbreak of the Civil War, he was put in command of USS *Crusader*, stationed in the Gulf of Mexico, and was able to keep several Union forts from falling into Confederate hands.

Later in 1861, Craven was promoted to the rank of commander and ordered to take the sloop of war USS *Tuscarora* to hunt for Confederate raiders operating in the Atlantic Ocean. While patrolling off the coast of Spain, he found the steam cruiser CSS *Sumter*, laid up for repairs in Gibraltar Harbor. *Tuscarora* and two other Union ships blockaded the raider for the next two months until its crew abandoned it. At this point, Craven was ordered back to the United States and given command of the monitor *Tecumseh*, which was stationed in the lower Chesapeake Bay area.

In 1864, the fatal moment arrived in the life of Tunis Craven. *Tecumseh* was ordered to join David Farragut's squadron in an attack on Mobile Bay. It should be noted that, following the capture of New Orleans in 1862—the battle in which Tunis Craven's brother Thomas Tingey Craven had fought so bravely—Mobile was the last major port in the Gulf of Mexico in Confederate hands. By 1864, almost all of the remaining trade between

Soldiers, Sailors and Marines

the Confederacy and the outside world passed through Mobile. Union commander Admiral Farragut's objective was to close the port as base for blockade running, once and for all.

Farragut was faced with a formidable challenge. The entrance to Mobile Bay was extremely narrow due to a series of barrier islands that stretched most of the way across the entrance to the bay. To make matters worse, Southern defenders had placed dozens of torpedoes (or mines) in the channel. The effect was to force the Northern fleet to sail close to shore, within easy range of the batteries from nearby Fort Morgan.

In recognition of his seniority, Tunis Craven, commanding officer of *Tecumseh*, was given the honor of leading the attack and firing the first shots in the battle that began on August 5, 1864. Commander Craven directed *Tecumseh* toward Confederate ram *Tennessee*, commanded by his former superior, Admiral Franklin Buchanan. The pugnacious Buchanan admonished his men to "whip and sink the Yankees or fight until you sink yourselves, but do not surrender." Disregarding a warning about the mines that lay ahead, Craven remarked, "I do not care a pinch of snuff about them." As the two ships approached each other, *Tecumseh* hit a mine, which exploded under its bow.

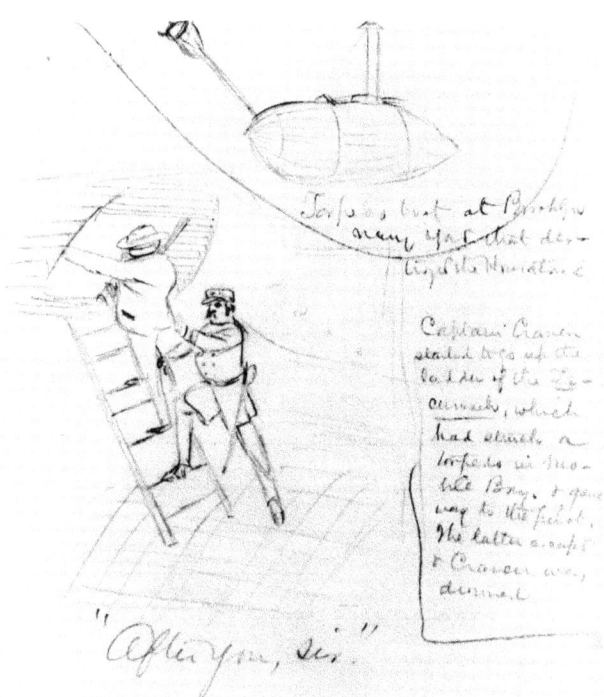

A sketch of Tunis Craven's heroic gesture as he bids his pilot to leave USS *Tecumseh* before it sinks. *Courtesy of Library of Congress, Prints and Photographs Division.*

Tecumseh began to sink rapidly, and Craven, who was in the pilothouse, ordered the men and officers in the compartment to evacuate the ship before heading for the escape hatch himself. At the foot of the ladder, he met the pilot, John Collins. Craven, knowing that it was not the pilot's fault they had hit a mine and that only one man could get out at a time, stepped aside and uttered the words, "You first, sir." Collins headed up the ladder and when he reached the top, he later recalled, "The vessel seemed to drop from under me." Craven and 93 of the 114 men were unable to escape from *Tecumseh*, which sank in less than a minute.

As *Tecumseh* sank, USS *Brooklyn*, commanded by Craven's boyhood friend from Portland, James Alden, stopped and reversed direction. This prompted Admiral Farragut's famous rebuke from his flagship, "Damn the torpedoes, full speed ahead." Moments later, Farragut received the following message from Alden, "Our best monitor is sunk."

The Confederate fleet, led by Admiral Buchanan's *Tennessee*, put up a good fight, but eventually they were overwhelmed by superior Union numbers and forced to surrender. Today, a buoy marks the spot in Mobile Bay where the heroic Commodore Tunis Craven went down with his ship. His body lies in thirty-eight feet of water.

The Marine: Charles Heywood

The Marine Corps originated as a military service at the beginning of the American Revolution when the Continental Congress authorized "two Battalions of Marines to be raised to serve on land and sea." Following the model of the British Royal Marines, American marines were considered "soldiers on shipboard." They were responsible for the security of their ship during battle, in addition to defending the ship's officers from possible mutiny. In the eighteenth and early nineteenth centuries, marines were mainly used as sharpshooters during combat and were stationed in the ship's "fighting tops" or masts.

As the United States Navy shifted from sail to steam power in the mid-nineteenth century, the mission of the Marine Corps changed, since without masts marine marksmen lacked a place from which to shoot. Although units of marines remained on shipboard, they were increasingly used as amphibious landing forces in military operations. Initially this was in the Western Hemisphere. Later, as American interests expanded, it was around the world.

Soldiers, Sailors and Marines

Early Career

Charles Heywood came along at a time when the role of the Marine Corps was in flux. He rose through the ranks to eventually become a major general and the ninth commandant of the corps from 1891 to 1903. During his tenure as commandant, the corps would change significantly.

Heywood was born in Waterville, Maine, in 1839. He was commissioned a second lieutenant in the Marine Corps in 1858 and stationed at the Brooklyn (New York) Marine Barracks. As a young officer, he was given a variety of assignments. He was first ordered to lead sixty-five marines to suppress the Quarantine Riots on nearby Staten Island. Next, he was sent on a special mission aboard the frigate USS *Niagara* to return captured slaves to Africa. Finally, in 1860, he was ordered to Central America to prevent the notorious filibuster, William Walker, from attempting another unauthorized expedition.

Civil War Duty

When the Civil War broke out, Heywood, now a first lieutenant, saw frequent action. He commanded a detachment of marines in the Battle of the Hatteras Inlet, off the North Carolina coast, which led to the capture of Confederate Forts Clark and Hatteras. During the winter and spring of 1861–1862, he participated in several amphibious operations on the James River during the Peninsula Campaign. Following this, he had the unpleasant but important job of blowing up the Norfolk Navy Yard to keep it from falling into Confederate hands.

Heywood's most noteworthy achievement during the Civil War occurred when he was aboard the sloop of war USS *Cumberland* off Hampton Roads, Virginia. On March 8, 1862, the Confederate ironclad *Virginia*, formerly and better known as *Merrimac*, attacked *Cumberland*, in an attempt to break the Union blockade, which had cut off Richmond and Norfolk from the outside world.

The historic first battle of ironclads between *Merrimac* and *Monitor* is well known. What is less well known is that the day before the celebrated engagement, *Merrimac* had attacked and destroyed *Cumberland* and *Congress*, two Union wooden-hulled vessels. Heywood, now a captain, was in command of *Cumberland*'s after-gun deck division.

Merrimac first attacked *Cumberland* and fired a devastating broadside into the ship, killing nine men in Heywood's division. The ironclad then proceeded to ram the hapless wooden vessel, which began to sink. Naval

The sinking of USS *Cumberland* by CSS *Virginia*, formerly USS *Merrimac*. Her gallant commander, Captain George Morris called on his crew to "give them a broadside boys, as she goes." *Courtesy of the Beverly Robinson Collection, U.S. Naval Academy Museum, Annapolis, Maryland.*

academy professor Charles Lewis wrote an account of what happened in his book, *Famous American Marines*:

> *The* Cumberland *had received her death-blow, and immediately commenced to sink. With her deck a shambles of wreckage, dead and wounded the crew continued to fire guns that were still serviceable. Heywood fired the last gun in the engagement and jumped overboard as the ship went down with her flag still flying.*

For his conduct, Heywood was brevetted (a temporary promotion) to the rank of major. *Cumberland*'s Captain George Morris wrote to Secretary of the Navy Gideon Wells about Heywood's "gallant conduct, and whose bravery upon the occasion of the fight with *Merrimac* won my highest applause."

After this adventure, the newly promoted major was employed in a fruitless, Atlantic Ocean-wide search for the infamous Confederate raider *Alabama*. This lasted until January 1864 when he was ordered to report for duty on USS *Hartford*. It was aboard *Hartford*, the flagship of Admiral David Farragut's Gulf Coast squadron, that Heywood would again distinguish himself. This time it was in the Battle of Mobile Bay.

Soldiers, Sailors and Marines

An 1862 French lithograph of the battle between ironclads *Monitor* and *Virginia* (*Merrimac*). The drawing is inaccurate since the wooden ships *Cumberland* and *Congress* had been destroyed by *Virginia* the previous day. *Courtesy of Naval Historical Center.*

On August 5, 1864, as *Hartford* entered the mine-filled channel leading to Mobile Bay, the ship was badly damaged by more than twenty shells from the Confederate ships and forts guarding the passage. Heywood, who was in command of a detachment of marines, received a commendation and a promotion for his "gallant conduct" in helping defend his ship and subsequently capture the Confederate ram *Tennessee*.

After the battle, Heywood was brevetted lieutenant colonel and ordered to occupy nearby Fort Powell with his troops. Lieutenant Colonel Heywood returned home late in 1864 and spent the remainder of the war on shore duty in Brooklyn, Philadelphia and Washington. Shortly after the war, he married Caroline Bacon, the daughter of a prominent Washington, D.C., businessman.

From Colonel to Commandant

Following the war, Heywood served as Admiral Farragut's fleet marine officer on board his flagship USS *Franklin*. In 1867, while on the European Station, Farragut made what historians consider a farewell cruise to the major ports of Europe. He visited twelve countries, from Russia in the Baltic Sea to Turkey in the Mediterranean Sea. At each stop, Farragut was received with enthusiastic acclaim. As one of his top aides, Heywood was also a participant in the ceremonies honoring the famous old admiral.

Heywood's life as a marine officer continued to be eventful. In 1873, he commanded a detachment of one thousand marines in Key West, Florida, in anticipation of a war with Spain, which fortunately never materialized. Three years later, the East Coast of the United States was paralyzed by a major rail strike. Lieutenant Colonel Heywood was ordered to take a battalion of marines to Baltimore, where they assisted the army in patrolling the streets and dispersing angry strikers attempting to destroy railroad property. Heywood then took his men to Philadelphia and later to Reading, Pennsylvania, to guard railroad stations and depots from further violence.

In 1885, Heywood and two battalions of marines were sent to Panama during a revolution to protect American lives and property. Heywood's actions received high praise from his commanding officer. "Your departure from the Isthmus gives me occasion to express my high estimation of your marine Battalion. You and your men have done hard and honest work. When conflict has seemed imminent, I relied with confidence on your body of soldiers."

Long identified with the liberal element in the marines, Heywood reached the pinnacle of his career in January 30, 1891, when he was appointed commandant of the corps. He was promoted to brigadier general in March 1899, by a special act of Congress, and to major general in July 1902.

At the time Heywood assumed command, the Marine Corps consisted of 75 officers and 2,100 enlisted men. During the more than twelve years that he held the post, he was instrumental in introducing a number of important changes, not the least of which was expanding the size of the corps to 7,800 officers and men. One of his major reforms was to establish a series of schools for potential officers as well as a regular system of examinations for their promotion.

Throughout his administration (1891 to 1903), Heywood realized the importance of working harmoniously with the navy. He worked constantly to improve the efficiency of the corps to make it an essential auxiliary to the Navy. One immediate benefit of this was that, with the support of the Naval Department, he was able to resist attempts by Congress to disband the corps.

At the same time, paradoxically, the Marine Corps was seeking to achieve a separate identity in regard to its mission and funding. Today, the secretary of the navy continues to oversee both the Marine Corps and the navy, although the commandant of the marines is a member of the Joint Chiefs of Staff.

As a result of the Spanish-American War (1898), the United States gained colonies in both the Caribbean and the Pacific. With the development of an

Soldiers, Sailors and Marines

The attack on San Juan Hill during the Spanish-American War. General Heywood's marines were involved in the amphibious operation. *Author's collection.*

American overseas empire, General Heywood foresaw a changing role for the marines. The Boxer Rebellion in China (1898–1901) further illustrated the importance of developing a mobile marine force to protect American interests around the world.

General Charles Heywood retired on October 3, 1903, as commandant of the Marine Corps after forty-five years of distinguished service. He died in 1915 and was buried in Arlington National Cemetery. Without exaggeration, it can be said both literally and figuratively that the man from Waterville, Maine, brought the Marine Corps into the twentieth century.

Chapter 4

Three Islanders Go to War

Thus far, this book has emphasized the careers of Maine's wartime governors as well as some of the state's generals and admirals who distinguished themselves while fighting for the Union cause. It is time now to examine the lives of three enlisted men. Charles Gray, Lafayette Carver and Woster Vinal were from Maine's islands. Although they were islanders, their reasons for volunteering, their combat experiences and their observations while on and off the battlefield were similar to those of young men everywhere.

Deer Isle's Charles Gray

In 1861, Deer Isle had a population of 3,600 people, approximately 600 of whom were young men between the ages of seventeen and thirty-five. The island had become a prosperous fishing center, and "every man who could afford it owned a boat," wrote Vernal Hutchinson in *A Maine Town in the Civil War* (1957). Although communications with the mainland were tenuous, island residents were very much aware of the looming threat of war. Hutchinson tells us that "every literate citizen" had read *Uncle Tom's Cabin*.

When the news of Fort Sumter arrived, the big question was, how would President Lincoln react? Upon hearing of his call for seventy-five thousand volunteers, a sigh of relief swept across the island, and it was hoped that the rebellion would soon be over. Hutchinson makes the point that, to the people of Deer Isle, indeed, to people throughout the North, the war was regarded as an armed rebellion. According to him, "it was a mad uprising of a few misguided states, to uphold slavery, to destroy the Union by sheer hatefulness."

Mainers in the Civil War

Corporal Charles Gray was killed at the Battle of New Bern on March 14, 1862. He was the first man from Deer Isle to join the army and the first from the island to die in the war. *Courtesy of the Deer Isle–Stonington Historical Society.*

In 1861, twenty-seven-year-old Charles Gray was a fisherman and the son of a sea captain. His family lived on North Deer Isle along Reach Road leading to Oak Point. Gray was on board a fishing schooner in Gloucester, Massachusetts, when he heard the news of Fort Sumter on April 13. After talking it over with a friend, the two young men left their ship, and on April 15, they enlisted for three months in the Eighth Massachusetts Infantry Regiment. As soon as they received their new uniforms, they had their pictures taken to send to their families back home.

Vernal Hutchinson gives us a description of Charles Gray: "He had long, black curly hair. He was muscular and of medium height. A finger was missing from his left hand, bitten off by a schoolmate in a fight long years before. Honest, fearless, happy-go-lucky he was just the type of lad the nation needed in her crisis."

Gray remained with the Eighth Massachusetts until his three months were up. He then returned to Deer Isle, where he found many of his friends had joined Maine regiments and his mother was "frantic with worry." Hutchinson wrote, "She had known no peace of mind while he had been gone." When her favorite son spoke of reenlisting, she pleaded with him not to go back. Finally, and against his wishes, he promised her that he would not return to the army.

After spending a few weeks at home, however, Gray became restless and joined the crew of a fishing schooner. When he arrived in Boston, he heard that a new regiment was being formed. Gray was unable to resist the temptation for adventure and, in spite of the promise he made to his mother, he joined the Twenty-third Massachusetts Volunteer Regiment on August 27, 1861. It was just twenty-six days after he had mustered out of

Three Islanders Go to War

the Eighth Massachusetts Regiment. Charles listed John Webster, his sister Sarah's husband, as his next of kin, not wanting to alarm his mother.

In February 1862, Charles Gray's Massachusetts regiment was part of an amphibious assault on the weakly defended North Carolina coast. The Union army of twelve thousand men, under the leadership of General Ambrose Burnside, landed on Roanoke Island, just north of Pamlico Sound. After a month's delay, Burnside, now joined by a fleet of thirteen gunboats, prepared to move across Pamlico Sound, up the Neuse River and attack New Bern, the old colonial capital of North Carolina.

The Battle of New Bern was fought on March 14, 1862. Burnside's army of men from Massachusetts, Pennsylvania and Rhode Island defeated a brave but outnumbered Confederate force of 4,500 men. After four hours of desperate fighting, New Bern surrendered. The town, once called the "Athens of the South," would remain under Northern control for the rest of the war. The Confederates had 68 men killed, 116 wounded and 400 captured. Union casualties were 90 killed and 385 wounded. One of the Union deaths was Charles Gray, the first Deer Isle man to volunteer for the war and the first to be killed.

On March 20, 1862, Gray's brother-in-law, John Webster, received the following letter from the commanding officer of the Twenty-third Massachusetts Regiment.

Captain E.A.P. Brewster:

> *Dear Sir, It is with pain that I have to announce to you the death of your brother Charles Gray. By his good conduct and bravery while with me, he had risen to the rank of Corporal and had he lived I should have promoted him again...He was shot through the body at the Battle of New Bern and died instantly. I can speak of him with pleasure, as he was brave and true: a good soldier and a true friend. He is buried here and I shall send his effects home at the earliest opportunity. Tell his sister and mother that I sympathize with them deeply. He was one that I took a particular interest in and we were personal friends. A few minutes before, he had borne off in his arms his wounded companion, through the thickest of fire. He returned to fall himself. His last words were, "we will never give up."*

The Websters naturally were devastated, and Gray's sister Sarah was faced with the unenviable task of breaking the tragic news to her mother. Vernal Hutchinson wrote, "The town was stunned." More boys continued to enlist, however, as Deer Islanders realized they were dealing with not only a personal but also a national tragedy.

Charles Gray's personal effects were returned home. His promotion certificate was printed on heavy paper and stated in part: "Know ye, that reposing special trust and confidence in the Valor, Fidelity and Abilities of Charles H. Gray, I do hear by appoint him a Corporal in the 23rd Regiment of Massachusetts Volunteers. Given this 29th day of November, 1861." It was signed Colonel John Hurtz. There was also his gaudy hat and a little wooden cartridge box containing the bullet that had killed him, a .62-caliber slug weighing a little over an ounce. This was quickly hidden away in the attic and long forgotten.

The Gray's extended family also suffered heavily. Charles's first cousin, twenty-five-year-old John Gray, was wounded during the siege of Vicksburg in July 1863. Like so many casualties during the war, he succumbed to his wounds a few weeks later. Later that year, another relative, Solomon Gray, died from disease at New Orleans. He was forty years old and a regimental chaplain. Hutchinson tells us he was married and left a large family.

At the end of the war, in a poignant moment, Addison Payne came to North Deer Isle to pay his respects to Charles Gray's parents. Payne was the comrade whom Gray had carried to safety during the Battle of New Bern before returning to the battlefield to die. When Payne began to recount the experience, Vernal Hutchinson informs us, "hardened soldier that he was, Payne broke down and cried."

Vinalhaven's Lafayette Carver and Woster Vinal

Twenty-four-year-old Lafayette Carver and eighteen-year-old Woster Vinal were two young men from Vinalhaven who enlisted in the Nineteenth Maine Infantry Regiment in the summer of 1862. In all, 125 men from the island town joined the army, 24 of whom would not return. Both men were present at some of the most critical battles of the war, including Gettysburg, Fredericksburg, Chancellorsville, the Wilderness, Spotsylvania and Cold Harbor.

The Nineteenth Maine was mustered into service on August 25, 1862. At full strength, the regiment had 1,008 men: 969 enlisted and 39 officers, many of whom came from Maine's coastal towns and villages, including Vinalhaven. One of the most famous of all Civil War regiments was the Twentieth Maine, led by Joshua Chamberlain, which distinguished itself at the Battle of Gettysburg. As we shall see, however, the Nineteenth Maine runs them a close second.

Three Islanders Go to War

Like many young men going to war, Carver and Vinal wrote letters home asking for news, extra provisions and reflecting on their experiences. In September 1862, Woster Vinal wrote his father, David, asking for postage stamps and "when you get a chance would you send me some tobacco, a couple of handkerchiefs and two or three pair of stockings, I have only one pair." He went on to say, "I want all hands of you to write. Don't be afraid of your three cents." Evidently Woster was chiding his family about being too frugal to spend money for postage.

Lafayette Carver rose through the ranks from corporal to sergeant and then, in February 8, 1864, he was promoted to lieutenant by his commanding officer, Major General G.K. Warren. Carver wrote to his father, John, "I should write oftener if I could get paper, but it is scarce. Also I have a great many letters to write for boys in the hospital."

Woster Vinal was a member of the Nineteenth Maine Regiment. He died in 1937, the last-surviving Civil War veteran on Vinalhaven. *Courtesy of the Vinalhaven Historical Society.*

The Nineteenth Maine first came under fire in October 1862 at Middlebury, Virginia. William Whitman and Charles True, in their *History of Maine in the War for the Union*, wrote, "They behaved with the coolness and steadiness that has characterized the regiment in every action in which it was to be engaged." The regiment, which was a part of the Army of the Potomac, then marched to Fredericksburg, where they played a largely supporting role in the bloody battle that followed.

It was at Gettysburg that the men of the Nineteenth Maine achieved their greatest fame. On July 2, 1863, the regiment played a critical role in turning back a determined Confederate attack on the center of the Union on Cemetery Ridge, in the process suffering heavily. When the Confederates were finally driven back, the men of the Nineteenth charged after them,

Lafayette Carver was a member of the Nineteenth Maine Regiment and fought in many battles. He was mortally wounded at the Battle of Cold Harbor in 1864. *Courtesy of Vinalhaven Historical Society.*

taking over four hundred prisoners.

The next day, Lafayette Carver, Woster Vinal and other Vinalhaven men in the Nineteenth Maine crouched behind the remains of a stone wall near the center of the Union line on Cemetery Ridge. At 1:00 p.m., an artillery duel began, followed by a massive assault across a mile of open ground known to history as Pickett's Charge. When what was left of three Southern divisions reached the Northern army, their ranks were decimated, though there were still enough men left to hit the Union center with considerable force. The Nineteenth was ordered into the gap, and terrible hand-to-hand fighting occurred for the next ten to fifteen minutes until the Confederates were finally driven back. The two days of fighting were very costly to the Nineteenth Maine: 65 men were killed and 137 wounded of the 405 men present at the start of the battle.

After the battle, Lafayette Carver wrote his father, John Carver:

> *My health never was better; the boys are all in good spirits and believe we can lick the Rebs wherever we may find them. If you have money to spare I advise you to spend it on taking a trip for you have no idea of an army unless you see one. Take a trip to Gettysburg or some other battlefield. I think you will feel well satisfied with what it might cost.*

The war dragged on for Carver, Vinal and their island comrades. In May 1864, the regiment suffered heavily during the three-day Battle of the Wilderness. Two weeks later, the Nineteenth was again engaged, this time in the Battle of Spotsylvania. Historians Whitman and True described their situation: "in this bloody battle the Nineteenth encountered the enemy face to face for seven days and nights with severe loss of killed and wounded."

After hearing that his older brother Thaddeus had died at Port Hudson, Louisiana, Lafayette Carver wrote to his father:

> *Oh Father of God only spare my life to see the end of this war and to return home and live once more in a land of peace and harmony. How we will appreciate it after going through so much to gain it. The more I suffer for my country, the more I shall prize it in the future. If I never do survive I believe you can die happy in knowing and saying you gave two sons for your country's cause. Give my love to mother and tell her that I think of her often. Tell Amanda* [Lafayette's wife] *that I would have written her today if I had clean paper. Tell the conscripts to come and help us wind this thing up.*

The year 1864 brought more bad news to the Carver family. When his child died, Lieutenant Carver wrote the following letter to his commanding officer: "I have to request a fifteen days leave of absence to visit my home in Vinalhaven, Maine. Under circumstances that exist at home my presence is much needed. My only child has been taken away by death and my wife is now sick with the same disease."

Needless to say, Carver was given permission to visit his ailing wife, Amanda Pierce Carver, whom he had married shortly before enlisting.

Lieutenant Carver returned to fight in the Battle of Cold Harbor (May 31–June 12). To quote from Whitman and True: "The regiment occupied a position within fifty yards of the enemy lines and held a rebel battery in subjection, though suffering many casualties from the enemy's sharpshooters." One of the casualties was Lafayette Carver, who was shot through the right lung on June 1, 1864. Carver was taken to Douglas Hospital in Washington, D.C., where he died on June 22. He was twenty-six years old.

After Lafayette's death, his father, John Carver, brought his son's body home to Vinalhaven. The Carvers had now lost two sons fighting for the Union cause. They are buried in the Carver family cemetery on Vinalhaven.

On June 22, 1864, at the Battle of Jerusalem Plank Road near Petersburg, Woster Vinal and two other Vinalhaven boys, Alden Dyer and Joseph Norton, were captured and imprisoned by the Confederates. On June 25, James P. Mills, Woster's cousin, wrote his father, David Vinal, a letter, describing what happened:

> *I now write you a few lines to inform you about Woster. On the 22nd our division were in breast works in front of the enemy and in the afternoon*

the left of our line were attacked and broke so we were obliged to fall back on account of being flanked. A great many of our boys chose to stay in the pits and among them were Wos, Norton and Dyer. I almost wish I was with them. I am now the only old member left in our Company and I was never so lonesome in my life. There were about 600 of our Brigade taken prisoners. I shouldn't worry about Wos for he is better off even if he has but one meal a day for here it is nothing but flank and fight all the time. If you have a chance you had better let Dyer's folks know concerning him.

For the remainder of the war, Woster Vinal was sent to some of the worst prisons in the South, including the Libby Prison in Richmond and the infamous Andersonville prison in Georgia. At Andersonville, Vinal recalled, "It was very cold one night and eleven of our boys, those who were the weakest, froze during the night." Vinal was one of the lucky ones to survive. During the

Lafayette Carver's gravestone on Vinalhaven Island. The inscription reads: "Lieut. Lafayette Carver died in Douglass hospital, Washington, D.C. of wounds received in Battle of Coal [*sic*] Harbor, June 22, 1864, age 28 yrs." *Author's collection.*

Three Islanders Go to War

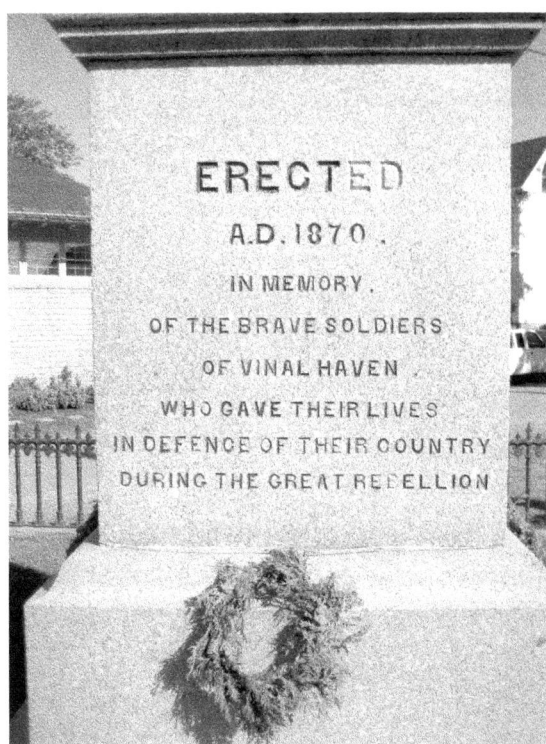

A Civil War monument on Vinalhaven's village green. The names of the twenty-four men who died in the "Great Rebellion" are inscribed on the monument. *Author's collection.*

fifteen months it was in operation, 12,900 of the 45,000 Union prisoners at Andersonville died of starvation, malnutrition, diarrhea or disease.

The war ended for Woster Vinal when he was released on April 28, 1865. He returned to Vinalhaven in a severely weakened physical and mental condition. As an older man, Woster contributed to *A History of the Nineteenth Maine Regiment.*

In it he recalled:

> *I have purposely omitted from this account the scenes of indescribable cruelty; suffering and horror in those awful prison pens. No one can know what our boys suffered except through bitter experience. It all comes back to me like an awful nightmare after all the years that have passed since the long months of hunger, sickness and brutality.*

Despite all the hardships he suffered, Woster Vinal lived until 1937 when he died at the age of ninety-three, the last surviving Vinalhaven veteran of the Civil War.

Chapter 5

Two Confederates

THE RAIDER: CHARLES READ

He had the audacity to sail into Portland Harbor with the intention of stealing a Federal ship. During a three-week rampage in June 1863, Charles Read captured or destroyed twenty-two Northern ships. Yet it is interesting that this diminutive, five-foot-one, twenty-three-year-old Confederate naval officer from Mississippi achieved his greatest notoriety for his unsuccessful raid on Portland, Maine.

Charles William Read was born in Yazoo County, Mississippi, in 1840. His father, William Read, was in constant debt, and in 1849, he left his family and headed west, hoping to improve the family fortunes in the California gold fields. It was not to be. Less than a year later, William died in Nevada City, California, leaving Charles the man of the family at age ten.

As a teenager, young Read ran away and joined the crew of a merchant ship until his mother, Maria, brought him home. Maria recognized that her restless son needed a more regimented, life, which she, as a widow with four younger children, was unable to provide. Accordingly, she petitioned her congressman to secure an appointment for Charles at the recently established United States Naval Academy. In 1856, Read was admitted, and his life changed forever.

At Annapolis, Read was an indifferent student, but he discovered that the military gave him a life of structure and routine that had a certain appeal. At the end of his four years, Charles was at the bottom of his class academically but near the top of the class in demerits. Along the way, he picked up the nickname "Savez," the one word from his French classes he was able to remember.

Charles Read found his calling while attending the United States Naval Academy. *Courtesy of Naval Historical Center.*

In *Sea Wolf of the Confederacy*, his biographer, David Shaw, wrote, "The United States Navy was a home for Read, an institution that grounded him more than at any other time in his life." When Mississippi seceded from the Union in January 1861, "Savez" Read resigned his commission and accepted a position in the Confederate navy. As a junior officer, he participated in a number of engagements in the Gulf of Mexico and on the Mississippi River during the first two years of the war. In 1862, when the commander of CSS *McRae* was mortally wounded in the battle to defend New Orleans, Read took command of the ship. His actions won him a reputation for daring and coolness under fire.

The Confederate Navy

It should be pointed out that the Confederate navy, such as it was, operated at a huge disadvantage throughout the war. In April 1861, the North had forty-two commissioned warships; the Confederacy had none. With few exceptions, the Confederacy was forced to wage a defensive war. Savez Read's offensive actions would make him one of the exceptions, according to another biographer, Robert Jones, in *Confederate Corsair*.

Jones goes on to describe the naval strategy the South used as similar to what the outnumbered United States Navy followed in the War of 1812. In that war, American privateers were issued commissions to attack British merchant ships. In the Civil War, Southern privateers were also called commerce raiders. Their objective was to disrupt the North's merchant fleet as much as possible. The fact that commerce raiders destroyed 5 percent of the North's merchant fleet was significant, however, and it was the early

Two Confederates

Throughout the war, Confederate raiders roamed the seas in search of Union merchant vessels. *Author's collection.*

twentieth century before the United States reestablished itself as a major world trader.

The Confederacy also went to great lengths to develop steam-powered ironclads to contest the Union navy on inshore waters. In 1862, Read was appointed executive officer of CSS *Arkansas*, an ironclad assigned to defend the key river town of Vicksburg on the Mississippi River. Although *Arkansas* was badly damaged and eventually blown up in the ensuing battle, the Union navy under David Farragut was forced to withdraw. Throughout the battle, Read's behavior impressed *Arkansas*' lieutenant, George Gift. "I think I have never looked at a person displaying such remarkable coolness and self-possession."

In January 1863, Read was ordered to Mobile, Alabama, where he joined CSS *Florida*, a swift, sleek warship, 190 feet long and one of a select group of "super" commerce raiders. Captain John Maffitt had heard of Read's "reputation for gunnery and determination at the Battle for New Orleans," and he wanted him as an officer on his ship.

Another "super" raider was the infamous CSS *Alabama*, commanded by the veteran officer Raphael Semmes. *Florida* and *Alabama* became renowned for their exploits. "Both were commissioned in 1862 and saw action through most of 1864, racking up thirty three and sixty four prizes respectively," according to David Shaw.

Six of the eight ocean-going commerce raiders, including *Florida*, were built by, or purchased from, the British by the Confederacy. Not surprisingly, this became a source of considerable tension between London and Washington, both during and after the war. The Southern raiders captured, burned or scuttled more than two hundred United States merchant vessels by the end of the war.

The mere presence of just a few commerce raiders on the high seas wrecked havoc on the United States shipping industry. Rates for insuring ships and their cargoes soared, with some estimates running as high as $9 billion in damages. Robert Jones states, "The raiders were the South's most successful use of sea power. By the end of the war, Great Britain surpassed the United States in cargo carried. The American merchant marine would not recover until World War One."

In January 1863, in the middle of a gale, *Florida*'s Captain John Maffitt ran past the Federal blockade of Mobile Bay. For the next three months, the ship captured or destroyed a dozen Northern merchant ships, including the clipper *Jacob Bell* bound for New York from China and carrying a cargo valued at $1.5 million. This would be the most valuable prize captured by a Confederate raider during the war.

Bermuda Harbor was filled with Southern blockade runners. *Author's collection.*

Two Confederates

An Independent Command

On May 5, 1863, *Florida* captured the brig *Clarence* off the coast of Brazil, carrying a cargo of coffee to Baltimore. For some weeks, Read had requested that Captain Maffitt give him a command of his own. The 250-ton *Clarence* provided the opportunity he was seeking, as we see in his letter:

> *Sir, I propose to take the brig which we have just captured and with a crew of twenty men proceed to Hampton Roads and cut out a gunboat or steamer of the enemy…Once in the Roads I would be prepared to avail myself of any circumstance which might present* [itself] *for gaining the deck of an enemy vessel.*

Maffitt agreed, "The proposition evinces on your part your patriotic devotion to the cause of your country." It is interesting that the entire crew volunteered to join Read on *Clarence*, which gave him his pick of the twenty best seamen. Maffitt gave him a small howitzer, wished him "God speed" and sent him on his way.

Clarence turned out to be a poor sailor. It took a month for the ship to lumber from Brazil to South Carolina, where on June 6, Read captured his first prize. Two days later, he captured another vessel. After interrogating their crew, he realized it would be too dangerous to carry out his original plan and enter the harbor at Hampton Roads. Meanwhile, the alarm was spreading that the "pirate ship" *Clarence* was in the area. Therefore, on June 12, the young captain switched his command to the next ship he captured, the bark *Tacony*, which had the added advantage of being larger and faster than *Clarence*. By the end of that week, Read and his crew had captured or destroyed six more vessels, including four in a single day.

A massive search for *Tacony* began, as several dozen ships put to sea from Hampton Roads, Philadelphia, New York and Boston. Read was accused of using unethical tactics because he induced his victims to stop by pretending his ship was a merchantman in distress. In Boston, insurance underwriters offered a $10,000 reward for *Tacony*'s capture. Meanwhile, the elusive raider slipped away into the fogs of the northeast, aided by bad weather.

As Read worked his way along the New England coast, "he left the blazing wrecks of seven [more] schooners and two other large merchantmen," wrote David Shaw. South of Nova Scotia, he captured the ninety-foot mackerel trawler *Archer*, along with four other fishing schooners, which he destroyed. By now Read realized that *Tacony* was too well known. In the past eighteen days, beginning on June 6, he had captured, bonded or burned twenty-one Union merchantmen. (By comparison, Captain Maffitt and *Florida* had captured or sunk twenty-one ships in four months.) Therefore, on June 24, the prudent Read transferred his flag to *Archer* and set fire to *Tacony*. As Read wrote in his log, "No Yankee gunboat would even dream of suspecting us. I therefore think we will dodge our pursuers for a short time."

Read considered his next move as he crossed the Gulf of Maine. *Archer* was a good sailor, but if he was to continue his quest, he needed to obtain a more suitable fighting vessel. Portland was an obvious target, but he knew little about the town. How was the harbor defended? Did it contain possible prizes?

On the morning of June 26, *Archer* came upon two men fishing south of Boothbay Harbor. Albert Bibber and Elbridge Titcomb were busily hauling the trawls that they had set the night before. Read realized they could probably provide the information he needed about Portland and hailed them to come alongside, but the fishermen ignored the demand and kept on with their work. At that point, Read lowered a boat to bring them aboard. Bibber and Titcomb suddenly found themselves confronted by five tough-looking sailors armed with knives and pistols. Their trawl lines were cut, and they were forced to board *Archer*.

Aboard *Archer*, Bibber and Titcomb weren't sure whether they were the victims of some drunken frolic or a smuggling operation. Brandy, cigars and twenty-dollar gold pieces calmed their fears, and they were taken below to be questioned by Read. Apparently he received the information he was looking for without revealing his real objective.

> *Off Portland I picked up two fishermen, who, taking us for a pleasure party, willingly consented to pilot us into Portland. From the fishermen I learned that the revenue cutter* Caleb Cushing *was in the harbor…I at once determined to enter the harbor at night to quietly seize the cutter and a steamer.*

The Raid

In *Confederate Corsair*, Robert Jones reminds us that, "to Portlanders, the war remained a distant conflict. The nearest known Confederates were five hundred miles away…No enemy ships had attacked Portland since the British burned the city in 1775." The citizens felt safe behind Portland's three forts—Fort Scammel, Fort Preble and Fort Gorges—which guarded the main channel. Each was bristling with guns, although, unknown to the Confederates, they were undermanned. On the advice of his engineer, Eugene Brown, Read shelved his original plan of also seizing a steamer. Brown had "expressed his doubts as to his ability to start the engines of the steamer proposed to be captured without the assistance of another engineer."

On the evening of June 26, the one-hundred-foot revenue cutter *Caleb Cushing* sat quietly at anchor in Portland harbor. *Caleb Cushing*'s captain, George Clark, had just died and his replacement, Lieutenant James H. Merryman, was expected the next day. In fact, as soon as Merryman arrived, *Caleb Cushing* would head to sea to hunt for *Tacony*. In the meantime, the ship was under the temporary command of Lieutenant Dudley Davenport, a Georgian who remained loyal to the Union cause. (Incidentally, Davenport and Read were classmates at the naval academy.)

About nine o'clock in the evening, *Archer* slipped into the harbor and anchored near the lightly manned *Caleb Cushing*. Most of the officers and a majority of the sailors were ashore on leave. Although *Caleb Cushing* was not originally designed as a warship, it had been remodeled by the Revenue Service and carried a thirty-two pound cannon. Read felt this would be a distinct improvement over the little howitzer he had been carrying since leaving CSS *Florida*.

At midnight, Read and two boatloads of heavily armed sailors left *Archer* and quietly rowed toward the nearby *Cushing*. The lone lookout hailed the approaching boats to "stand clear," but before he could sound the alarm, the Rebels swarmed aboard. Within five minutes, the crewmembers were in handcuffs. When the acting captain, Lieutenant Davenport, stumbled on deck to see what the disturbance was, he was also seized. Recognizing his former classmate, Read reportedly snapped to the Georgian, "You ought to be ashamed of yourself for deserting the South."

It was now after 1:00 a.m., and Read needed to get his prize out of the harbor before dawn and the authorities were alerted. Using the fisherman, Albert Bibber, as a pilot, he avoided the main channel, which ran past the three forts, and set a course for the far side of Hog Island (now called Great Diamond) and past the dangerous Cow Island ledges. Meanwhile, the wind had dropped, and Read was forced to put out rowboats to tow his prize. It was a tight squeeze, but they made it past the ledges into Hussey Sound. Then, at about 4:00 a.m., the Boston packet *Forest City* steamed past, carrying *Cushing*'s replacement captain, James H. Merryman.

Jedediah Jewett, Portland's customs collector, was eating breakfast when members of *Caleb Cushing*'s crew, who had remained on shore, notified him that their ship had put to sea. He immediately raised the alarm, assuming that the Southerner, Lieutenant Davenport, had run off with the ship to join Read. Mayor Jacob McClellan ordered the church bells rung, and hundreds of men headed for the waterfront. Reuben Chandler, baggage master of *Forest City*, described the scene: "Every man jack in Portland rolled up his sleeves and started for the dock armed with everything from ancient blunderbusses to cutlasses. Fishermen, stevedores and bakers, undertakers and teamsters, doctors and a college professor. By cracky, they were mad as hornets."

Jewett moved fast. He telegraphed the news to Federal agents in Boston and quickly chartered *Forest City*, *Chesapeake* and a smaller steamer, *Casco*, to go after the stolen revenue cutter. He then ordered artillery and soldiers to be sent over from nearby Fort Preble. At the docks, crowds of eager volunteers surged on board the seven-hundred-ton *Forest City*, forcing the captain to turn a fire hose on the mob to keep the boat from capsizing. As he was leaving, the captain asked the mayor for any further instructions. "Catch the damn scoundrels and hang every one of them," Mayor McClellan replied.

Off Cape Elizabeth, *Caleb Cushing* sailed southeast in a light breeze. About 11:00 a.m., the watch reported that two steamers were in sight, which caused Read to "clear for action." An onboard search revealed four hundred pounds of power but only five rounds for the thirty-two-pounder. (Lieutenant Davenport, still a prisoner on board, had refused to reveal where the shells were hidden.) As *Chesapeake* drew closer, *Cushing* opened fire. A few rounds were exchanged, none of which caused any damage. After pausing for a council of war, the two Union steamers headed toward the stolen cutter, intending to ram and board the less maneuverable vessel, still under sail.

Knowing that his crew would be overwhelmed by the mob of men on the approaching steamers, Read acted swiftly. In short order, he released the prisoners on board *Cushing*, set fire to his prize and abandoned ship. The Confederates rowed desperately away from the now-blazing revenue cutter in an attempt to escape before they were caught by *Forest City*. As they came alongside, Lieutenant Merryman realized that these were the men that the fleet of Federal ships had been vainly searching for. The first to board was a small man with a goatee who handed over his pistols and identified himself. "I am Second Lieutenant Charles W. Read, Confederate States Navy, Your prisoner sir."

At approximately 2:00 p.m. on June 27, the fire on *Caleb Cushing* reached the powder magazine, and Casco Bay reverberated with a tremendous explosion. A reporter from the *Portland Argus* wrote, "The smoke rolled up in vast columns, fragments of shells, masts and spars are seen hundreds of feet in the air. The cutter began to sink immediately." Charles "Savez" Read was finally caught, although he had destroyed his twenty-second ship.

Two Confederates

Read was imprisoned in Fort Preble before being transferred to Fort Warren in Boston Harbor. After repeated attempts to escape, he was returned to the Confederacy in a prisoner exchange where he continued to serve in the navy until the end of the war. Savez Read married in 1867 and raised three children. He died in 1890 of pneumonia in Meridian, Mississippi, at the age of fifty.

A General in Gray: Danville Leadbetter

What was a West Point graduate from a small town in Maine doing fighting for the Confederacy? Danville Leadbetter was born in Leeds, Maine, in 1811. He entered the United States Military Academy in 1832 and graduated in 1836, finishing third in a class of forty-nine. Second Lieutenant Leadbetter was briefly assigned to an artillery unit before being transferred to the Engineer Corps. His early appointments included supervising the construction of fortifications in New York harbor and serving as a member of a joint naval and engineering team that surveyed the country's defense needs on the Pacific coast.

Leadbetter was promoted to rank of captain in 1852. Although he didn't realize it at the time, his life would change dramatically that year when he was assigned to supervise the repairs of Fort Morgan and Fort Gains in Mobile, Alabama. Over the next few years, his duties included improving Mobile's harbor facilities, constructing a customs house as well as a lighthouse and repairing Mobile's marine hospital.

Like a number of Northern officers serving in the South for an extended period of time, Leadbetter began to identify with the attitudes and way of life in the South. In 1855, while in Mobile, he met and married a wealthy widow, the former Delphine Kennedy Hall. Leadbetter resigned his commission and moved into his wife's elegant mansion on Government Street in Mobile.

In 1857, Leadbetter was appointed as Alabama's chief engineer, a civil position. His primary responsibility was to improve the defenses around Mobile harbor. Ironically, one of his last official duties as a U.S. Army engineer had been to evaluate the defenses of the gulf coasts of Alabama, Mississippi and Texas.

When war broke out in April 1861, Leadbetter cast his lot with his adopted state and was commissioned a major in the Confederate army. By August, he was promoted to lieutenant colonel and made acting chief of the Bureau of Engineers. In this position, he was ordered to continue to strengthen the defenses of Mobile and other Gulf coast forts.

The Daniel Leadbetter house in Mobile, Alabama, where he lived before the war, following his marriage to the former Delphine Kennedy. *Courtesy of Museum of Mobile, Alabama.*

It is important to understand the critical lack of engineers in the Confederate army at the start of the war. In his book *Confederate Engineers*, James Nichols tells us, "Engineers amounted to but two percent of the officers and one percent of the soldiers." Furthermore, few of the officers, in what was to become the Confederate Corps of Engineers, had any previous military experience, although some had been trained at military academies. In this respect, as well as in many others, the North had a decided advantage over its opponent.

Suffice to say, the challenges faced by Confederate engineers were enormous. It was their job to plan and erect defenses, construct (and destroy) roads and bridges (mainly pontoon), to conduct topographical surveys during campaigns, to reconnoiter enemy works and to prepare and distribute accurate maps. Heavy equipment had to be purchased from foreign countries or captured from the enemy. Some could be manufactured, but the South's industrial capacity was very limited.

At first, Confederate president Jefferson Davis nominated only West Point graduates of high achievement to serve in the Engineer Corps. Danville Leadbetter was one of thirteen trained engineers that the Confederacy was

Two Confederates

fortunate to have on hand at the start of the war. (With one exception, these men had all finished in the top fifth of their classes that ranged in size from fifty to sixty cadets.) Aside from Leadbetter, very few were originally from the North.

Following his assignment at Mobile, Colonel Leadbetter was appointed acting chief of the Confederacy's Bureau of Engineers. At the same time, he was responsible for overseeing the repair and construction of railroad bridges and communication lines in eastern Tennessee. For a while, the overextended Leadbetter also commanded a brigade in the field with special orders to guard against sabotage.

A letter from Confederate secretary of war Judah Benjamin directed him to deal harshly with pro-Union insurgents in eastern Tennessee. In a response to Benjamin, Leadbetter reported, "Two insurgents have today been tried for bridge burning, found guilty and executed by hanging." Both men—Jacob Madison Hinshaw and Henry Fry—were executed near an old depot in Greeneville, Tennessee, and their bodies were left on public display for many hours as a warning to others.

That same day, Colonel Leadbetter issued a proclamation addressed to the citizens of east Tennessee: "Bridge Burners and destroyers of railroad tracks will be tried by drum-head court-martial and hung on the spot." Colonel Leadbetter was not without compassion, however. On one occasion, he pardoned a sixteen-year-old boy, "who was not very intelligent," and released him into the custody of his father.

The year 1862 was a busy one for the erstwhile Mainer. In February, he was promoted to brigadier general and given command of the Engineering Department of eastern Tennessee. His particular charge was to supervise fortifications around the key city of Chattanooga. Then, in the spring, he was sent to Virginia to help plan the defense of Richmond, which was under attack in what was known as the Peninsula Campaign. Back in Mobile in November, he used his skills to make that city one of the most strongly fortified in the Confederacy.

Danville Leadbetter may have been a good engineer, but he was a poor commander of troops in the field. In May 1862, while he was crossing the Cumberland Mountains in eastern Tennessee, a Federal force surprised his brigade. In a letter to his uncle, Confederate captain John Gibbons described the scene. "The first command the General gave was 'take care of yourselves boys,' and then he fled as fast as he could. The General was in a handcar on a railroad bridge and he ran into a crowd of retreating soldiers killing twenty and wounding thirty more. When he was safely across, he blew up the bridge thus cutting off the retreat of his own men except those who could swim across the Tennessee River. Once on his horse the old fool ran among his men and killed two or three more."

In 1863, General Leadbetter was responsible for laying out siege lines for Confederate general Braxton Bragg's attack on Chattanooga. The lines ran along Missionary Ridge and Lookout Mountain, which overlooked Chattanooga, now occupied by Northern troops. The poor placement of some of these lines helped lead to an eventual Union victory, though Leadbetter's responsibility is not clear. Shortly before Union forces successfully attacked Confederate positions, Leadbetter was withdrawn and sent to advise General James Longstreet on the siege of Knoxville.

The unsuccessful, eighteen-day siege of Knoxville ran from November 17 to December 4, 1863, and is considered a pivotal moment in both the war and in the career of Danville Leadbetter. Leadbetter's advice was considered invaluable, since he had designed Knoxville's fortifications the previous year. The fifty-two-year-old Leadbetter arrived with the message to Longstreet that General Bragg wanted him to "attack very promptly."

Longstreet had already sealed off the approaches to Knoxville, hoping to starve the garrison into submission. He and Leadbetter then spent three days reconnoitering the Union lines, which was a costly delay, according to Longstreet's chief artillery officer, General Porter Alexander. As we shall shortly see, Alexander was highly critical of other advice General Leadbetter gave to Longstreet.

Leadbetter recommended, and Longstreet agreed to, a direct assault on Fort Sanders, which they considered the weak link in the Union lines surrounding Knoxville. The result was a disaster of the first magnitude. The Rebel offensive bogged down in a twelve-foot-wide by ten-foot-high ditch. With no scaling ladders and in the face of heavy fire, the attack failed within twenty minutes. Confederate casualties were 813; Federal losses were 5 dead and 8 wounded.

In his biography of Longstreet, Jeffry Wert writes, "Fort Sanders was a tragic debacle and for this Longstreet bears responsibility." In his memoirs, General Alexander added, referring to plans for the assault, "Some of its features were crazy enough to have come out of Bedlam… Leadbetter evidently had no appreciation of the ground…I will go to my grave believing that Leadbetter devised and imposed it on Longstreet, who afterward preferred to accept the responsibility rather than plead that he had let himself be taken in."

When Longstreet heard that General Bragg had been driven from Chattanooga, and that Union general Sherman was advancing from the

Two Confederates

Leadbetter is buried next to his wife in Magnolia Cemetery, Mobile, Alabama. His body was brought from Canada, where he died in 1866. *Courtesy of Museum of Mobile, Alabama.*

south, he lifted the siege and withdrew his army into winter quarters in northern Tennessee. Leadbetter, suffering from ill health, returned to Mobile, where he remained for the rest of the war.

General Leadbetter's legacy to the Confederacy is mixed. Military historian Ezra J. Warner says in *Generals in Gray* that "he was highly thought of by his superiors," yet General Alexander's charge that he "robbed Longstreet of victory at Knoxville" cannot be dismissed. Then, of course, there was the railroad bridge disaster.

Danville Leadbetter was one of seventeen Confederate generals who fled to Mexico at the end of the war to avoid capture. The next year he moved to Clifton, Canada, where he died in 1866 at the age of fifty-five, an exile from his family and his adopted state. Today, Leadbetter lies beside his wife in the Magnolia Cemetery in Mobile, Alabama.

Chapter 6

Three Daughters of Maine

We often hear the remark that "these are days that try men's souls." I think they try women's souls too. I shall remember you and all the noble women of the North when this land is at peace.
—Abraham Lincoln, addressing a gathering of nurses in Washington, D.C., shortly before his assassination in 1865.

What role did women play in the Civil War? In spite of poor records kept on the activities of women, Lynda Sudlow, in her book *A Vast Army of Women: Maine's Uncounted Forces in the American Civil War*, tells us "the names of over one hundred Maine women who took an active role in the Civil War have been uncovered," and more are added every year as letters, diaries and memoirs are discovered.

It is important to remember that, in the middle of the nineteenth century, there was a great deal of resistance to women working outside the home, especially in time of war. A precedent was set, however, by Florence Nightingale, who led a team of thirty-eight nurses in the Crimean War in the 1850s. Although women served mostly as nurses in the Civil War, some joined their husbands on the battlefield, where they acted in supportive roles. Casual physical exams at the time allowed others to disguise themselves and fight beside the men in their regiment. Lynda Sudlow tells us that there are four hundred documented cases of women serving as soldiers. If a female soldier was discovered, however, she was sent home in disgrace.

According to Jane Schultz, a professor of English and women's studies at Indiana University, in addition to three thousand nurses, thousands more women were employed as cooks, matrons, laundresses, seamstresses, waitresses and chambermaids. When the work was arduous, however, most of the workers were African American. Nearly half of all the cooks and laundresses hired by the Union army were African Americans.

In 1861, President Lincoln appointed Dorothea Dix, from Hamden, Maine, superintendent of Union army nurses. One of her standards for nurses was that they be "plain-looking and middle-aged." Although nicknamed "Dragon Dix," she established the army's first professional nursing corps during the course of the war. Numerous Maine women left the state and joined the nursing corps. One was Amy Bradley, who was a teacher before she became a nurse. Another was Mary Kneeland, from Byron, Maine, who was a nurse and a spy and was said to be "more dangerous than a regiment of soldiers," according to Lynda Sudlow.

Then there was twenty-one-year old Augusta Foster, who was found to be "too handsome" to be a nurse. Augusta followed her husband, Charles, into the army when he joined Maine's Fifth Infantry Regiment. She soon came to be known as Daughter of the Regiment. This was an honorary term and appears to have been bestowed on many young women who did everything from nursing to joining men in battle. In Augusta's case, she had a horse shot out from under her during the first Battle of Bull Run. Shortly afterward, she left the regiment and spent the rest of the war working in a hospital in Washington, D.C. Augusta never saw her husband again.

THE WRITER: HARRIET BEECHER STOWE

Harriet Beecher Stowe was perhaps the best-known woman in the country during the Civil War era. Her connection with Maine is less well known. Stowe's husband, Calvin, was teaching at Bowdoin College when she wrote the provocative and internationally famous bestseller *Uncle Tom's Cabin*. Although Harriet was born in Connecticut, her influence on the prewar period was so profound that we may consider her a Daughter of Maine because of her book. James M. McPherson writes, "It is not possible to measure precisely the political influence of *Uncle Tom's Cabin*. Yet few contemporaries doubted its power."

Harriet came from stern Puritan stock. Her father, the Reverend Lyman Beecher, was a fiery Congregationalist minister who was preaching in Litchfield, Connecticut, when Harriet was born in 1811. She was the seventh child, and fourth daughter, in what would eventually be a family of eleven children. When Harriet was four her mother died, leaving the family devastated.

Three Daughters of Maine

According to one of her seven brothers, "Harriet was an odd, undersized, inward child, slouching and daydreaming while others talked." Harriet worshiped her father. What she enjoyed most as a child was reading, especially in her father's study. It was there that she also was able to watch him work on his sermons. Father and daughter were also alike in that they were incapacitated by periods of depression throughout their lives.

When Lyman Beecher remarried, it was the eldest Beecher daughter, Catherine, Harriet's older sister by eleven years, who took care of the children, not the new stepmother. Harriet was sent to a local school until, at twelve, she was enrolled in the Hartford Female Seminary, founded by Catherine. By the age of sixteen, Harriet was also a teacher at Hartford Female Seminary.

Harriet Beecher Stowe became a world-famous author following the publication of *Uncle Tom's Cabin*. *Courtesy of Facts on File, Inc.*

In 1832, Lyman Beecher was named president of the Lane Theological Seminary in Cincinnati. Most of the children, including Catherine and Harriet, accompanied him. By the spring of 1833 the enterprising Catherine had established the Western Female Institute where she and Harriet served as coprincipals. Although Harriet realized the importance of education for young women, she was personally ambivalent. Barbara White points out in *The Beecher Sisters* that Harriet resented the amount of time she had to spend on her "school duties." "I can not visit much nor read for amusement or write half of what I wish to," she wrote a friend. By 1833, she had already published *Geography for Children* as well as stories and sketches in various magazines. *A New England Sketch*, published in 1834, won her a prize of fifty dollars.

In 1836, Harriet married a widower, Calvin E. Stowe. She had become friends with his wife, Eliza, and, following Eliza's early death, she and Calvin drew closer. The scholarly Stowe came from New England and had been valedictorian of his class at Bowdoin College. When Harriet met him, he was a professor of biblical literature at the Lane Theological Seminary. In the 1830s, Lane Seminary was a hotbed of abolitionism and Stowe an ardent critic of slavery and a supporter of the Underground Railroad. Over the years, the Stowes frequently hid runaway slaves in their home, since Cincinnati was just across the Ohio River from Kentucky.

Calvin Stowe was nine years older than his twenty-four-year-old, rather plain wife. Nearsighted and balding, he was hardly a romantic figure himself, although he was reputed to have a good sense of humor. The marriage was not an easy one, but Calvin always supported his wife's career as a writer. In turn, she was able to help him when he slipped into periods of self-doubt, which were frequent.

Harriet had no trouble bearing children. Nine months after they were married, she produced twin daughters, followed by two boys in 1838 and 1840. Motherhood brought her little joy, she confided to a friend. "I am a mere drudge with few ideas beyond babies and housekeeping."

The young Mrs. Stowe did not give up her dream of becoming a writer, and the family certainly needed any extra money she could earn. In 1838, she hired a German girl to help with her growing family, which gave her several hours a day to write. In 1843, Harper & Brothers published a collection of her stories entitled *The Mayflower: Sketches of Scenes and Characters among the Descendants of the Pilgrims*.

The Stowe family continued to expand. By 1850, Harriet had three more children, one of whom died as an infant. Seven children in fifteen years left her exhausted. "I am sick of the smell of sour milk, and sour meat and sour everything. Of clothes that would not dry, and of a moldy stench everywhere." In 1846, she retreated to Brattleboro, Vermont, where she spent ten months at a water cure establishment, which improved her health and spirits.

Harriet had never particularly enjoyed the "rough country" atmosphere of Cincinnati, and when Calvin was offered a job at his alma mater, Bowdoin College, in 1850, she was thrilled. Although perpetually tired and in the middle of her seventh pregnancy, she journeyed east with her family and set up housekeeping in the comfortable coastal town of Brunswick. This would be the location for the writing of *Uncle Tom's Cabin* and Harriet Beecher Stowe's emergence as a major literary figure.

Three Daughters of Maine

The Harriet Beecher Stowe house in Brunswick, Maine. Stowe wrote *Uncle Tom's Cabin* while her husband was teaching at Bowdoin College. *Courtesy of the George M. Mitchell Department of Special Collections & Archives, Bowdoin College Library, Brunswick, Maine.*

The immediate background for the book was the passage of the Fugitive Slave Law, which was part of the Compromise of 1850. The law declared that runaway slaves must be returned to their owner instead of being helped to escape. It was nicknamed the "Bloodhound Law," since dogs were often used to track down runaway slaves. Anyone suspected of harboring slaves was subject to six months' imprisonment and a $1,000 fine. The final straw was the provision that a black person suspected of being an escaped slave was not eligible for trial. The result was that many free blacks were conscripted into slavery.

The Fugitive Slave Law brought home the question of slavery to Northerners, since it made each individual responsible for enforcing the "peculiar institution," as this euphemism for slavery was called in the South. Moderate abolitionists were upset. Others like the Beecher family, including Harriet, were outraged.

The Beecher brothers denounced the controversial law from their pulpits (all seven were ministers). At the same time, Harriet's friends were urging her to write about the issue. One version of the book's origins was that it followed the death of her eighteen-month-old son Samuel from cholera; Harriet had a vision of a dying slave, and she was determined to focus her story on "life among the lowly." She began to write, drawing on her personal experiences with slavery, which included visiting a plantation when she was living in Cincinnati. Her research included talking with ex-slaves, including Frederick Douglass, to validate the accuracy of her story.

On June 5, 1851, the *National Era* magazine published the first of forty installments, which ran until April 1852. In 1889, her youngest son, Charles, wrote in a biography of his mother, "It had been contemplated as a mere magazine tale of perhaps a dozen chapters, but once begun it could no more be controlled than the waters of the swollen Mississippi." Harriet agreed, "I could not control the story; it wrote itself."

Her narrative was immediately popular, although Harriet received only $300 for the serialized magazine version. In 1852, at the suggestion of Mrs. John P. Jewett, wife of the publisher, *Uncle Tom's Cabin* was published as a two-volume set. At this point, the Stowe family had to make a business decision. John P. Jewett offered them a choice between jointly sharing the costs and profits or taking a 10 percent royalty on each copy sold. They chose the latter option, which meant a check for $10,000 arrived at the end of three months. It was more money than her husband could have earned in years and ended the genteel poverty they had endured.

The novel was a sensation. Barbara White wrote, "In Brunswick with her sisters, Harriet Beecher Stowe seemed stunned. The situation would have been overwhelming for any fledgling author." The first printing sold out within a few days. (And this was before any reviews had appeared.) Publisher John Jewell kept three presses going twenty-four hours a day. He sold 10,000 copies the first week and over 300,000 the first year. It was eventually translated into all major languages, as well as Finnish and Hindu.

Millions of her books were sold around the world, although Mrs. Stowe saw little personal profit due to the unauthorized copies that were printed outside the United States. It was later adapted to the stage and was a smash hit, although again the Stowe's did not receive a penny in royalties. According to some reports, *Uncle Tom's Cabin* became the second best-selling book in history after the Bible. It is still in print today.

Accolades poured in, and Mrs. Stowe was fêted both at home and abroad. The poet, Henry W. Longfellow wrote, "I congratulate you most cordially on the immense success and influence of *Uncle Tom's Cabin*. It is one of the greatest triumphs recorded in literary history." Henry James called it "much less a book than a state of vision." When she traveled to England, where the book sold even better than in the United States, crowds everywhere cheered her. The Duchess of Sutherland gave her a gold bracelet, and she dined with

Three Daughters of Maine

Charles Dickens, William Thackeray and Prince Albert. She was praised by George Sand in France and in Russia by Leo Tolstoy.

Not surprisingly, the reaction in the South was not as cordial, as the book was essentially banned. Barbara White tells us that when a British visitor gave a copy to a young Southerner, he was run out of town. The book was called a distortion, and Stowe was called, "a vile wretch in petticoats, a liar", and a "loathsome person." The *Southern Quarterly Review* said her foul imagination had produced a book "whose touch contaminates with its filth."

This is not the place to summarize *Uncle Tom's Cabin*. Suffice to say that Mrs. Stowe was attempting to communicate the pain and suffering of slavery by showing how different kinds of slaveholders, including the notorious Simon Legree, treated the Christlike Uncle Tom. To the modern reader, the book feels overly sentimental and melodramatic, with stereotypical images of black people: the faithful Uncle Tom, the pickaninny, etc. The real importance of the novel, however, was that it awakened the country to the evils and immorality of the slave system.

During the war, Harriet continued to focus her attention on the emancipation of slaves. Abolitionists were upset with the lack of progress in this area and criticized Lincoln for not addressing the issue more forcefully. There were charges that the president had been "bought off." Harriet's brother, Henry Ward Beecher, harangued the president for "dragging his feet." In 1862, Harriet decided to confront Lincoln directly.

The title page for the 1852 edition of *Uncle Tom's Cabin. Courtesy of the George M. Mitchell Department of Special Collections & Archives, Bowdoin College Library, Brunswick, Maine.*

It was when she was in Washington, ten years after the publication of *Uncle Tom's Cabin*, that Harriet Beecher Stowe finally met President Abraham Lincoln. When they were introduced, the president is supposed to have said, "So you're the little lady who wrote the book that started this great war." Like a number of famous quotations, doubts have been cast as to whether Lincoln actually made the statement. Apparently he did not realize whom he had met until his wife reminded him that she was the famous Mrs. Stowe.

On January 1, 1863, she was attending a New Year's celebration in a Boston theater when the news arrived that the Emancipation Proclamation had been signed. Harriet was sitting in the balcony, and the crowd called for her to come to the rail. Her biographer, Forrest Wilson, described the scene: "The audience shouted and waved, she bowed and wiped tears from her eyes. Thus ended the cycle that had begun with her vision in a Brunswick church."

From 1862 to 1884, Mrs. Stowe produced, on average, a book a year, which supported several impecunious family members as well she and her husband. Calvin died in 1886, and a few years later, her mind began to go. In 1893, she wrote to Oliver Wendell Holmes, "My brain is tired out." Harriet Beecher Stowe died in 1896 in Hartford, Connecticut.

Barbara White provides us with an appropriate epitaph: "No matter what happened to her for the rest of her life, she would know that she had helped bring an end to slavery"

THE HUMANITARIAN: DOROTHEA DIX

Miss Dix was the stateliest woman I ever saw and she was very dignified in manner and conversation. She was tall, straight as an arrow and unusually slender.
—*Nurse Annie T. Whittemyer, 1865*

If Harriet Beecher Stowe was the most influential woman connected with Maine during the Civil War era, Dorothea Dix runs her a close second. During a lifetime (1802–1887) that spanned most of the nineteenth century, Dix distinguished herself in three careers. She was a teacher, a social reformer and, finally, during the Civil War, she was a nurse.

Dorothea Dix was born in the frontier town of Hamden in the middle of what was then the Maine wilderness. Her Harvard-educated father, Joseph, was an itinerant Methodist preacher who neglected his wife and young children and drank too much. Her mother, Mary, suffered from depression and was unable to cope with their impoverished existence. As the oldest of three children, the burden of caring for her younger brothers fell on young "Dolly." She often described her family life as "non-existent. I never knew childhood." However, Dolly credited her father with teaching her to read.

When the War of 1812 broke out, the family fled to Vermont and then to Worcester, Massachusetts. At the age of twelve, Dolly left her dysfunctional family and went to live with her well-to-do paternal grandmother at the Dix Mansion in Boston. The seventy-year-old grand dame tried unsuccessfully to turn her granddaughter into a lady by hiring a dance instructor and a seamstress to attend to her needs. After two difficult years, the exasperated old woman sent the rebellious girl to live with an aunt in Worcester. (The final straw may have been when Dolly was caught giving away food and clothes to poor children at the mansion's front gate.)

Dorothea Dix was superintendent of nurses during the Civil War. *Courtesy of Facts on File, Inc.*

In Worcester, she met Edward Banks, her older cousin by fourteen years, who was a prominent attorney. Edward suggested she open a "little dames school," since girls were not allowed to attend public schools. The next year, the fifteen-year-old Dorothea opened a school for elementary school–age girls. She appears to have been a good teacher, although she was a strict disciplinarian.

Edward continued to encourage her teaching career. At the same time, he became increasingly smitten with his young cousin. When Dorothea was eighteen, the thirty-one-year-old Edward confessed he had fallen in love with her. A flustered Dorothea closed the school and returned to Boston, ostensibly to care for her elderly grandmother.

A year later, Edward proposed marriage to his nineteen-year-old cousin. She accepted but would not commit to a wedding date. Their engagement was broken off the next year. The reasons for this are unknown. Did her parents' unhappy marriage bring back bitter memories? Dorothea was an attractive young woman and would continue to have suitors into her forties. She had, however, apparently made a decision not to marry. Instead, she focused on her teaching career and improving her own education by attending lectures by Harvard professors and devouring the books in the library of her Harvard-educated grandfather.

In 1822, with her grandmother's enthusiastic support, Dorothea opened a school for girls from well-to-do families on the grounds of the Dix Mansion in Boston. With the additional income, Miss Dix was now able to bring her recently widowed mother and younger brothers to live with her. The school became popular and mirrored its founder's personal views. Emphasis was placed on the natural sciences, especially botany, and on the development of a strong moral character.

Dorothea ran the school from 1822 to 1836. During this time, she also wrote nine books, ranging from children's stories to devotional texts to an anthology of poetry. Her bestseller, *Conversations on Common Things* (1824), reached its sixtieth edition in 1869. Miss Dix suffered frequently from poor health, however, and in 1836, she reluctantly gave up her life as an educator. Lynda Sudlow, in *A Vast Army of Women*, describes her as "nervous, delicate and over strained with incipient lung trouble."

While living in Boston, Dorothea had joined the congregation of liberal Unitarian theologian Dr. William Channing, who subsequently became a good friend. During a previous health crisis in 1830, she had accompanied the Channing family to St. Croix in the Virgin Islands as a tutor for his children. On her return, she found that a friend, General Levi Lincoln, had become governor of Massachusetts and that his secretary of state was her cousin and former fiancé, Edward Banks. The two, along with Channing, would later provide invaluable aid in helping her pass mental health legislation.

In 1836, at the age of thirty-three, Miss Dix's health again broke down. Following Dr. Channing's advice, she set sail for the warmer climes of the Mediterranean. She got as far as England before her worsening condition forced her to stop. At an estate near Liverpool, Dorothea spent a year recovering at the home of a wealthy Unitarian merchant and philanthropist, William Rathbone, a friend of Dr. Channing. Rathbone was a Quaker and a prominent humanitarian, and through him, Dorothea was introduced to the world of social reform. She observed British prison conditions and became familiar with new theories for caring for the "mentally disordered," as such people were called.

Three Daughters of Maine

The Social Reformer

Back in Massachusetts, Dorothea agreed to teach a Sunday school class for women inmates in the East Cambridge House of Correction. It was a turning point in the life of the thirty-nine-year-old woman who, up to that point, was known primarily as a dedicated teacher. She was horrified by what she saw. Prostitutes, drunks, criminals, retarded persons and the mentally ill were jammed together in unheated, foul-smelling cells. In the "dungeon," she found people considered insane chained to the wall, sleeping on the floor. When she asked "why," the jailer answered, "Lunatics do not feel the cold and fires would be unsafe." One of her first responses was to launch a campaign to have stoves placed in cells and have inmates properly clothed.

Miss Dix then spent two years investigating prisons and hospitals throughout Massachusetts. Every place she visited brought new evidence of neglect and cruelty. One poor soul had been chained in a closet for fourteen years. The popular belief was that such people were incurable and that living in such miserable conditions made no difference to them.

Everywhere she went, Dorothea made careful notes and compiled a report that she called a *Memorial*, which she presented to the Massachusetts legislature: "I proceed Gentlemen, to call your attention to the present state of insane persons confined within this Commonwealth in cages, stalls, pens! Chained, naked, beaten with rods and lashed into obedience." With the support of influential friends like the educational reformer Horace Mann and the persistent force of her arguments, Miss Dix was able to persuade the Massachusetts legislature to appropriate funds to expand the state's mental hospital in Worchester.

Dorothea next investigated conditions in Rhode Island, Connecticut and New York. After presenting her *Memorial*, she was able to secure funds from each legislature for new facilities. In 1844–1845, she went to New Jersey, where she overcame bitter opposition and helped to establish the state's first mental hospital in Trenton. For the next three years, frequently in poor health, she traveled thousands of miles, visiting literally every state east of the Mississippi River and two Canadian provinces. Her tactic was the same everywhere. She rarely spoke in public but made her case by writing her *Memorial* and choosing her supporters wisely, including members of the press.

Typically, Miss Dix would remain in a state until the legislature had appropriated the necessary funds for new, or improved, facilities. In all, she played a major role in founding thirty-two mental hospitals, including one in Maine, fifteen schools for the mentally deficient, a school for the blind in Illinois, a hospital in Nova Scotia and numerous training facilities for nurses. She also was instrumental in establishing libraries in prisons and mental hospitals.

Miss Dix's ideas for more humane treatment for the mentally ill were considered radical, and she attracted a following among enlightened politicians and doctors in each state. Her name became a household word as she slogged over rough roads from state to state, frequently suffering from lung trouble and the susceptibility to malaria.

In 1848, Miss Dix moved to the national level and began a vigorous campaign for the appropriation of funds for the care of the insane and the benefit of "the blind, deaf and dumb." She continued her politicking for six years, until 1854, when both houses of Congress approved the measure. Sadly, President Franklin Pierce vetoed the bill, which he said exceeded the powers of the federal government and therefore was unconstitutional.

Worn out by thirteen years of lobbying, argument and travel, Miss Dix headed for Europe and a well-earned rest. The "rest" quickly turned into fact-finding expeditions across England and the European continent. She inspected jails and almshouses in fourteen countries, some as distant as Greece, Turkey and Russia. Within two years, Dix had effected changes in the way that European countries dealt with the mentally ill, the same process that had taken well over a decade in the United States.

Superintendent of Nurses

With the outbreak of the Civil War, sixty-year-old Dorothea Dix offered her services to the surgeon general. On June 10, 1861, she was appointed superintendent of women nurses, with orders to "select and assign women to general or permanent military hospitals." She would later say, "This is not the work that I would have my work judged by." She was autocratic and intolerant, poor qualities for such an important administrative position.

Controversy erupted when she refused to accept qualified nuns as nurses. Then there was her famous dictum, issued to eliminate 'flighty' women and those seeking a husband: "All nurses are required to be plain women. Women under thirty need not apply. Dresses must be brown or black with no adornments, and no hoop skirts." Suffice to say these restrictions caused a wail of anguish and in time were ignored. Perhaps this is where the term "Dragon Dix" came from.

Miss Dix was opinionated, and she played favorites. Sophronica Bucklin was a vivacious young woman who was accepted as a nurse in spite of her youth. After the Battle of Gettysburg, she requested permission to go to the

Three Daughters of Maine

Campbell General Hospital, formerly the Union Hotel, was one of the many military hospitals in Washington. *Courtesy of Print and Picture Collection, Free Library of Philadelphia.*

battlefield where nurses were desperately needed. Miss Dix refused to give her permission until the determined young woman said she was going anyway. At that point, the "kind superintendent forgave me," wrote Sophronica.

When Superintendent Dix visited hospitals, she often dismissed volunteer nurses she had not personally approved. She frequently came into conflict with army doctors, "who were determined to give her no foothold in the hospital where they reigned." In fairness, however, we should mention that her even-handed treatment of Union and Confederate wounded brought her grudging respect from many Northerners and admiration from the South.

As time went on, Miss Dix's influence and power were diminished. In 1863, Secretary of War Edwin Stanton sharply reduced her role by granting the surgeon general, as well as Miss Dix, the power to appoint nurses. In August 1864, Georgy Woolsey and her sister, Caroline, were asked to go to Philadelphia to help organize a new hospital. Georgy later wrote, "We had a good natured laugh over a visit from Miss Dix, who, poor old lady, kept up the fiction of appointing all army nurses. When she found us already established she gave us permission without having spoken with either of us."

Miss Dix's Civil War accomplishments are most significant for her work in establishing nursing as a legitimate career for women. One of her biographers, Helen Marshall, wrote, "The years that followed were to witness steady improvement in the training of nurses and in the care of patients. Medical schools were to recognize psychiatry not as a mere handmaiden of medicine, but as a 'legitimate daughter,' a science worthy of a special place in the curriculum."

Dorothea Dix would resume her peripatetic life of visiting hospitals and prisons, particularly in the South, where so many facilities had been damaged. At the age of eighty, she retired to an apartment on the grounds of the New Jersey State Hospital, which she had established thirty-five years previously. Although a virtual invalid, she continued her crusade for the mentally ill, writing letters from her bed until her death in 1887.

THE "SAINTLY" CARPETBAGGER: AMY MORRIS BRADLEY

Equally obnoxious and pernicious is it to have Yankee teachers in our midst, forming the minds and shaking the instincts of our youth, sewing the seed of their poisonous doctrine upon the unfurrowed soil.
—Wilmington Dispatch, *March 8, 1867*

She was called the "Saintly" Carpetbagger for her work as an educator in Wilmington, North Carolina, following the Civil War. As the above sentiment indicates, do-gooders from the North were not welcome in the South. According to one old-timer, "Swarms of riffraff from northern cities poured into the South. Among them were female missionaries with a holier-than-thou attitude. 'Do it our way' said those arrogant New England schoolmarms." Amy Bradley, fresh from her nursing achievements in the war, would soon change the minds of Southern mothers who were determined that their children would not go to a Yankee school.

Amy Bradley was born in 1823 in the tiny farming village of East Vassalboro, Maine. Unlike Harriet Beecher Stowe and Dorothea Dix, Amy spent a considerable amount of time in Maine during the course of her life. The youngest of eight children, she learned to be self-reliant when her mother died when Amy was six. By the time she was thirteen, her older siblings had all married, leaving Amy alone with her sixty-three-year-old father. At that point, her father also departed to remarry, leaving others to bring up his youngest daughter.

Three Daughters of Maine

The cottage in East Vassalboro, Maine, where Amy Bradley was born and grew up. *Courtesy of Dianne C. Cashman.*

    For the next few years, Amy lived with different family members in nearby towns, attending school whenever she could. At age fifteen, she embarked on her career as a teacher, while continuing to study at the local high school. She worked first in small "dame" schools before moving on to a district school in East Vassalboro. In 1844, she got a break when she was appointed principal of a grammar school in Gardiner, Maine, with the charge to restore discipline. Her biographer, Diane Cashman wrote in *Headstrong* that the twenty-one-year-old "Miss Bradley did not traumatize; she mesmerized. Within two weeks the scholars were in perfect order. The overseers pronounced both pupils and principal 'quite satisfactory.'"

    In 1847, Miss Bradley took a job at Boston's Winthrop School, where she quickly established herself as a demanding teacher with little need for the switches and whips used by other teachers. Evenings and weekends she read, visited museums and attended lectures by "some of the most distinguished men in Massachusetts," according to her journal. Amy had a social life, including a serious beau at one point, although she was acutely aware of her lack of a formal education. At the same time, she remained the dutiful daughter and returned frequently to Maine to visit her father, who had returned to Gardiner with a new wife.

    During one visit, Amy's pallid, listless appearance so alarmed her family that her new stepmother urged her to visit her brother's family in the warmer climate of Charleston, South Carolina. After considerable thought,

Amy resigned from Winthrop School and, in October 1850, boarded a ship for the voyage south. The weather in Charleston was certainly warmer, but Amy was shocked by the city's "self assured image," wrote Diane Cashman. It had "an air of decay," Amy commented in her journal.

Not surprisingly, Miss Bradley was horrified at witnessing slavery first hand. "Slavery!" she wrote in her journal. "Shall I look upon this fearful system in a more favorable light after this visit in the South? NO! God forbid! My heart recoils from it as from a dreadful poison. Being an eyewitness tends to strengthen my aversion to this system in all its forms." Although Amy recoiled from "the peculiar institution" (slavery) and the Southern way of life, her health had improved when she returned to Maine six months later.

Amy's health continued to suffer, however, making it impossible for her to resume her teaching career. At age thirty, she decided to accept a job as a governess for a wealthy family in Costa Rica. This was partly to enjoy the benefits of warmer weather and partly to escape persistent family urgings that she find a husband.

Amy's monthlong journey to Costa Rica is a story in itself. She experienced a series of adventures that began with a harrowing voyage to the Caribbean in an old side-wheeler, "I lay in my berth vomiting for four days." A brutal crossing of the mosquito-infested Nicaraguan isthmus followed, including a forty-mile mule ride over treacherous mountain trails amid drenching rains. Amy survived the trip, though she was suffering from malaria by the time she arrived at the coffee plantation where she was to be a governess and tutor.

Governess Bradley soon realized the limitations of the job, resigned her position and headed for San Jose, the capital of Costa Rica. Within three months, she had established Costa Rica's first English school, and in six months, she had become fluent in Spanish. As Diane Cashman says, "Amy could be a charismatic teacher in any language and it didn't take long for her school to win a fine reputation." She stayed in San Jose for almost four years until news of her father's worsening health brought her home.

The Civil War Nurse

With the outbreak of the Civil War, Amy—following the Dorothea Dix pronouncement that "nurses should be plain looking and over thirty"—volunteered her services as a nurse. Her administrative abilities were quickly noticed, and she was named superintendent of a brigade hospital in Alexandria, Virginia. As has been noted in the introduction to this section, despite the efforts of Florence Nightingale, the importance of nursing was not valued at the time. Nurse Amy Bradley had to deal not only with filthy conditions but resentful and frequently intoxicated surgeons, dismissive generals and a lack of medical supplies.

Undaunted, Nurse Bradley rolled up her sleeves and went to work. She and her staff transformed unsanitary, makeshift first-aid stations into clean, well-run hospital tents. Diane Cashman tells us that Amy found her calling working as a nurse for the Army of the Potomac during the Peninsula Campaign in 1862. Bradley served on hospital ships transporting wounded from the battlefield. She assisted with amputations and with prisoner exchanges. She wrote letters for soldiers to their families. In the process, she frequently ran into old friends and former students from Maine, who naturally were delighted to see her. Whatever free time Nurse Bradley had, she visited hospitals in the Washington area, and in the spirit of Dorothea Dix, she frequently suggested improvements.

Union general George Meade, the future victor at Gettysburg, met Amy shortly before he left on the Peninsula Campaign in 1862. Hearing that she was accompanying them, he responded, "Well Miss Bradley, if I am wounded I shall tell them to send me to your hospital."

Primitive ambulance wagons were used to transport wounded Union soldiers from the battlefield to hospital ships. *Author's collection.*

A few months later, as Union troops were withdrawing from their unsuccessful assault on the Richmond peninsula, the renowned landscape architect, Frederick Law Olmstead, was put in charge of evacuating fifteen thousand sick and wounded Union soldiers. (As a civilian, Olmstead had gained a reputation as a superb organizer and administrator.) Amy was superintendent of nurses aboard the one-thousand-patient hospital ship *Ocean Queen*. In a letter to a colleague, Olmstead wrote, "As for the women, Mrs. Howland, Miss Woolsey and Miss Bradley—if every man on the ship was their brother, I should have said such untiring industry, self possession and tranquil cheerfulness was incredible. It beats all I ever imagined of women or experienced."

In December 1862, Nurse Bradley was transferred to an unsanitary convalescent camp of five thousand men, popularly known as "Camp Misery," near Alexandra, Virginia. Lynda Sudlow writes in *A Vast Army of Women*: "Into this hellish place Amy Bradley went to do what she could to improve conditions. It was a tremendous undertaking. Everything she had done previously paled in comparison." Sudlow tells us that she devised an efficient system for distributing food, clean clothing and blankets and how she obtained certificates for soldiers whose pay was in arrears. She even purchased a bathtub for those who were able to bathe themselves. In 1863, Frederick Knapp, president of the U.S. Sanitary Commission, wrote, "Miss Bradley has the confidence and cooperation of all the officers in charge of the camp…Miss Bradley shows what an amount of work can be done by one individual with the resources at hand."

Nurse Bradley's hectic schedule finally wore her down, and she was forced to take a few weeks off. On her return, in addition to her other duties, she decided to publish a weekly camp newspaper, the *Soldiers' Journal*. Camp newspapers were good for morale, but men had previously staffed them. Miss Bradley raised $550.00 to buy a printing press, which convinced camp officials she was equal to the job. The first issue appeared on February 17, 1864, and cost $0.05. The paper generated considerable proceeds and went to a fund for Union orphans.

Soldiers' Journal ultimately had twenty thousand subscribers and was filled with useful information for convalescing soldiers, such as how to apply for pensions or artificial limbs. It also included war news and literary offerings by Amy herself. By the end of 1864, President Lincoln, Vice President Hannibal Hamlin and General Grant were among the *Journal*'s subscribers. She was called the "soldiers' friend," and when the camp was broken up, her grateful patients presented her with a gold watch.

Three Daughters of Maine

The "Saintly" Carpetbagger

At the end of the war, a group of prominent Boston Unitarians formed a philanthropic organization, The Soldiers' Memorial Society (SMS), whose purpose was to establish free schools for poor children in the city of Wilmington, North Carolina. After a rest in Maine to recover her health, Amy offered her services to the group and was appointed the official SMS agent in Wilmington.

It was in Wilmington that Amy achieved the greatest triumph of her long and distinguished career. She arrived in Wilmington on December 30, 1866, and was faced with a chilly reception. Town officials told her that her mission would never succeed—something she had already heard from her disillusioned SMS predecessor. Adversity was nothing new to Amy Bradley, and as she toured the battered old city, embittered residents ignored her or even spat as she passed by. Wilmington's population of eighteen thousand had suffered greatly during the war, and for a time, Amy was regarded as simply another Northern carpetbagger.

Miss Bradley soon became a familiar figure on the Wilmington streets as she toured the city in early January to drum up interest for her free school. After four days, she had three pupils; by January 15, 1867, she had fifty students. Two months later Amy had achieved a miracle. The school was full and had a long waiting list. Diane Cashman writes, "The Bradley approach to education worked. Well fed scholars who were treated with dignity and motivated by creative teaching behaved themselves and paid attention."

Newspaper hostility continued into March (see the quotation at beginning of this section), though by mid-1867, Amy had the support of the mayor and the town's leading citizens. Wilmington's grateful populace raised $1,000, which—combined with contributions from other sources—allowed Amy to open another school building. After two years, the venture had grown from 3 students and a single teacher into a school system, with eight teachers and 435 students housed in three buildings.

It is difficult not to overemphasize Amy Bradley's role as the founder of Wilmington's public school system. To quote Lynda Sudlow, "Despite initial opposition, her methodology gained widespread acceptance. She became known as a pioneer educator and her school was a stunning success." In 1904, thirty-seven years after her arrival, Amy Bradley died in Wilmington at the age of eighty-one. In recognition of her educational achievements, flags flew at half-staff throughout the city.

In 1976, a K-12 private school was founded in Wilmington and named the Amy Bradley School. In keeping with Amy's philosophy of education, the school emphasizes a noncompetitive, academic approach to learning.

Soldier's Monument, Lewiston, Maine. Before Governor Samuel Cony left office in 1867, he wanted to ensure that Maine's veterans received proper recognition for their sacrifices in the war. Accordingly, during the next generation, statues were erected in towns all over state. On October 15, 1866, the Lewiston City Council appropriated $5,000 for a monument that was financed by municipal funds. The image seen here is taken from *Harper's Weekly* 12 (April 25, 1868).

The monument was designed and executed by Franklin Simmons, a sculptor of national note and a native of Lewiston. The granite pedestal is eleven feet high and the bronze figure is six feet, nine inches tall. On the base of the monument are the names of the 112 officers and men from Lewiston who gave their lives in the Civil War. The Lewiston Soldier's Monument was dedicated on February 28, 1868, and is thought to be the first that was built in the state. It still stands in front of the City Hall Building in Kennedy Park in the center of Lewiston. *Courtesy of the Maine Memory Network.*

Bibliography

Cashman, Diane Cobb. *Headstrong: The Biography of Amy Morris Bradley*. Wilmington, NC: Broadfoot Publishing Company, 1990.

Clark, Charles E. *Maine: A History*. Hanover and London: University Press of New England, 1990.

Craven, T.T. *Testimony Taken in the Trial of Commodore T.T. Craven*. Ithaca, NY: Cornell University Library, 1992.

Dannett, Sylvia G. *Noble Women of the North*. New York and London: Sagamore Press, 1959.

Dow, Neal. *The Reminiscences of Neal Dow*. Portland, ME: Evening Express Publishing Company, 1898.

Duncan, Roger F. *Coastal Maine: A Maritime History*. Woodstock, VT: Countryman Press, 2002.

Eicher, John H., and David J. Eicher. *Civil War High Commands*. Stanford, CA: Stanford University Press, 2001.

Ferguson, Eugene S. *Truxtun of the Constellation: The Life of Commodore Thomas Truxtun, U.S. Navy, 1775–1822*. Baltimore, MD: Johns Hopkins University Press, 1956.

Hale, John. "The Maverick Governor from Bangor." *Bangor Daily News*, December 9, 1992.

Headley, J.T. *Farragut and our Naval Commanders*. New York, NY: J.T. Tract & Co. 1867.

Hunt, H. Draper. *Hannibal Hamlin of Maine*. Syracuse, NY: Syracuse University Press, 1969.

Hutchinson, Vernal. *A Maine Town in the Civil War*. Freeport, ME: Bond Wheelwright Co., 1957.

Bibliography

James, Edward T., ed. *Notable American Women 1607–1950: A Biographical Dictionary*. Cambridge, MA: Belknap Press of Harvard University Press, 1971.

Jones, Robert A. *Confederate Corsair*. Mechanicsburg, PA: Stackpole Books, 2000.

Jones, Terry. *Historical Dictionary of the Civil War*. Lanham, MD: Scarecrow Press, Inc., 2002.

Keegan, John. *The American Civil War*. New York: Alfred A. Knopf, 2009.

Lewis, Charles Lee. *Famous American Marines*. Boston, MA: L.C. Page and Company, 1950.

Marshall, Helen. *Dorothea Dix: Forgotten Samaritan*. New York: Russell & Russell, 1937.

McPherson, James M. *Battle Cry of Freedom*. New York, NY: Oxford University Press, 1988.

Nichols, James L. *Confederate Engineers*. Tuscaloosa, AL: Confederate Publishing Co., 1957.

Purcell, L. Edward, ed. *Vice Presidents*. New York: Facts on File, Inc. 1998.

Read, Charles. "Reminiscences of the Confederate States Navy." *Southern Historical Society Paper* 2, no 5 (1876).

Rich, Louise Dickinson. *The Coast of Maine*. Camden, ME: Down East Books, 1975.

Rowe, William Huthinson. *The Maritime History of Maine*. Gardner, ME: Harpswell Press, 1989.

Shaw, David W. *Seawolf of the Confederacy*. Dobbs Ferry, NY: Sheridan House Inc., 2005.

Smith, Mason Philip. *Confederates Down East*. Portland, ME: Provincial Press, 1985.

Stover, Arthur Douglas. *Eminent Mainers*. Gardiner, ME: Tilbury House, 2006.

Sudlow, Lynda. *A Vast Army of Women*: Maine's *Uncounted Forces in the American Civil War*. Gettysburg, PA: Thomas Publications, 2000.

Trulock, Alice. *In the Hands of Providence. Joshua Chamberlain and the American Civil War*. Chapel Hill: University of North Carolina Press, 1992.

Waldrup, Carole Chandler. *The Vice Presidents*. Jefferson, NC, and London: McFarland Co., Inc., 1996.

Warner, Ezra J. *Generals in Blue: Lives of Union Commanders*. Baton Rouge: Louisiana State University Press, 1964.

———. *Generals in Gray, Lives of Confederate Commanders*. Baton Rouge: Louisiana State University Press, 1959.

BIBLIOGRAPHY

Wert, Jeffry D. *General James Longstreet*. New York: Simon & Schuster, 1993.

White, Barbara. *The Beecher Sisters*. New Haven, CT, and London: Yale University Press, 2003.

Whitman, William E.S., and Charles H. True. *Maine in the War for the Union*. Lewiston, ME: Nelson Dingley Jr. & Co., 1865.

Williams, Charles E. *The Life of Abner Coburn*. Bangor, ME: Press of Thomas W. Burr, 1885.

Wilson, James Grant, and John Fiske, eds. *Appleton's Cyclopaedia of American Biography: Six Volumes*. New York: D. Appleton & Co., 1888–1889.

Zinnen, Robert O., Jr. *City Point: The Tool That Gave General Grant Victory* (Spring 1991).

ARCHIVAL MATERIALS CONSULTED AT THE FOLLOWING LOCATIONS:

Free Library of Philadelphia, Philadelphia, Pennsylvania.
General Henry Knox Museum, Thomaston, Maine.
Maine Historical Society, Portland, Maine.
Maine Maritime Museum, Bath, Maine.
Patton Free Library, Bath, Maine.
Portland Public Library, Portland, Maine.
Rockland Historical Society, Rockland, Maine.
Rockland Public Library, Rockland, Maine.
Vinalhaven Historical Society, Vinalhaven, Maine.
Vinalhaven Public Library, Vinalhaven, Maine.

About the Author

Harry Gratwick is a lifelong summer resident of Vinalhaven Island in Penobscot Bay. A retired history teacher, Gratwick had a forty-six-year career as a secondary school teacher, coach and administrator. He spent most of these years at Germantown Friends School in Philadelphia, Pennsylvania, where he chaired the History Department and coached the baseball team.

Harry is an active member of the Vinalhaven Historical Society and has written extensively on maritime history for two Island Institute publications, *The Working Waterfront* and *Island Journal*. *Mainers in the Civil War* is his third book about Maine. Harry's next book, *Shipping Lanes, Stories from the Maine Coast*, will be published in the spring of 2012.

Gratwick is a graduate of Williams College and has a master's degree from Columbia University. Harry and his wife, Tita, spend the winter months in Philadelphia. They have two grown sons, a Russian daughter-in-law and two grandsons.

Visit him at www.harrygratwick.com.

Also by Harry Gratwick:
Penobscot Bay: People, Ports and Pastimes
Hidden History of Maine

Visit us at
www.historypress.net

www.ingramcontent.com/pod-product-compliance
Lightning Source LLC
Chambersburg PA
CBHW042144160426
43201CB00022B/2400